We are truly

OVERCOMER

Redeemed Masterpiece

Elite Foundation® Publisher
Ft. Lauderdale, Florida

**Inspired Stories of Real People
with Unconquerable Will to Thrive
and Be Alive**

Published by Elite Foundation®, Fort Lauderdale, Florida

Book Cover: Jesus Cordero

Editorial Review: Elite Literary Team

Elite Foundation® is a registered trademark

Printed in the United States of America.

ISBN: 978-1-7320778-8-1

Published by Elite Foundation®, Fort Lauderdale, Florida

This publication is designed to provide accurate and authoritative information regarding the subject matter covered. It is sold with the understanding that the publisher is not engaged in rendering legal, accounting, clinical or other professional advice. If legal advice or other expert assistance is required, the services of a competent professional should be sought. The opinions expressed by the authors in this book are not endorsed by Elite Foundation and are the sole responsibility of the author rendering the opinion.

Most Elite Foundation® titles are available for bulk purchases for sales promotions, premiums, fundraising, and educational use. Special versions or book excerpts can also be created on direct request for specific needs aligned with Elite Foundation®

For more information, please write:

Elite Foundation® Publisher

2003 West Cypress Creek Road, Suite 103
Ft. Lauderdale, Florida 33369

Or email: ElitePublisher@EliteFundsFreedom.org

Visit us online at: www.EliteFundsFreedom.org/book_program

Elite Foundation is a 501(c)(3) nonprofit organization that offers Indie publishing services to impact lives and community. When you Invest in Yourself, you Fund Freedom. Royalties from all our goods and services support scholarships/grants and the work done with victims and survivors of human exploitation and sex trafficking. Elite Foundation's vision is to eradicate the aftermath experienced by victims by creating a future for every survivor.

OVERCOMER

"Let perseverance finish its work so that you may be mature and complete, not lacking in anything."

~James 1:2-4

The culmination of the inspirational Elite four-book series is Overcomer. In this text you will learn of the fibers and stitches that were woven together through some of the hardest life experiences a person can endure. The types of experiences that unfortunately occur with significant frequency, but always in darkness and kept silent. That is until now.

Thank you to each of the brave souls, who have bared it all for you, the reader, to be spared what they went through, in order to learn the wisdom from their experiences. Each author is a testimony to the spirit of survivorship and the best of humanity.

The truth is each of us was created for a divine purpose, before we set one foot, or took our first breath, on this earth. Our lives are a journey that sometimes takes us to places we never fathomed or desired, we are faced with the shortfalls of humanity, and we even make choices in free-will that lead us towards pain. But God, in infinite grace loves us unconditionally, gives hope and instills faith, which resonate at the highest of frequencies and leads us to unwavering will to not only thrive but to be fully alive, present and intentional in this world.

OVERCOMER

The book titled Overcomer was written during one of the worst global virus pandemics experienced, Covid-19 turned the world upside down, and changed our global and national culture, seemingly overnight. We were asked and then mandated to exercise physical distancing and then extended quarantine. Millions were infected, hundreds of thousands lost their lives to the virus, and our economies were dramatically depressed. The already marginalized were left in dire circumstances and the most unsavory among us were given unprecedented access to our children and vulnerable adults on and off line. Yet, amidst this chaos each writer albeit challenged, rose up against the compounded adversities, and did not deter from sharing their truth with you.

We have and will continue to be refined through this shared pandemic experience. There is a new beginning arising in the twentieth century that will bring forth the fruit of our labor amidst the famine of despair. It will bring unity, as most of us have never experienced, and the paradigm of life and work balance, will adapt. The earth and its inhabitants will begin to flourish again but this time in expectant confidence in God.

As you read the pages of this text you will be drawn into stories of powerfully overcoming hardship, loss, physical and emotional pain, exploitation, and trafficking. At times the read is not an easy one, but the one promise made by all the collaborating authors is that you will be forever changed, if you commit to execute the shared wisdom and realize that you are a masterpiece.

The intent of our work, whether it be perceived from the context of self, work or humanity, is to ignite and engage, in order to affect the actualization of personal and community transformation through actionable faith, hope and unconditional love.

Elite Authors are disruptors, change agents, who seek excellence in pursuit of the audience of One. Influencers and Thought Leaders, who value the importance of compassion, generosity and integrity, while employing courage from within, to invest in others. Socially-conscious individuals, who have achieved in life and business, but not without the realizations that result from living. It is these very unique, but collective experiences, that contribute to what is known about the experience of being redeemed to be a masterpiece, a Warrior for Change.

"When you find your definitions in God, you find the very purpose for which you were created. Put your hand into God's hand, know His absolutes, demonstrate His love, present His truth, and the message of redemption and transformation will take hold."

~Ravi Zacharias

Dr. Jessica Vera, Ph.D.
Award Winning Multiple Bestseller
Elite Foundation Founder/CEO

Table of Contents

OVERCOMER

PART I

Escaping the Grip

CHAPTER 1

Pushed to The Frontlines

By Tiffany Jacobsen

My name is Tiffany and I am a believer who has struggled with my identity in Him and self-worth. My life did not start out easy, but God, he never left my side (Deuteronomy 31:6). Most people are welcomed into this world when they are born, that may have been the case for a short time. But my story is far from waking up as a child in the loving arms of a father and mother. My parents were both addicts, at one point in my life they were trafficking me and drugs. My innocence was taken at an incredibly young age by them and the people they partied with. My worth was already diminished, my innocence robbed by the very ones that were supposed to protect me. Eventually my dad left, and my mom had me until the age of two…until one day she chose to not want to be a part of my life either. She chose drugs over me.

Who was this little girl nobody wanted, who was she, that people thought they had a right to take my innocence?

The day came when a neighbor heard this little girl crying, she called the police saying that nobody had been in that home for weeks and there was a girl inside the house. The cops came and found this girl in the corner, legs crossed, soiled diaper, blanket and teddy bear, legs stuck crossed because that was the position of protection after violations took place. So, at an early age I learned I was unwanted and worthless, not worth protecting. This, I believe was the time when God had been my 911, he protected me under the shadow of his wings until the police found me. (Psalm 91)

The day they found me was the day you would think I would be brought somewhere safe. That is not how my journey evolved. They had called my dad who had moved to Wisconsin and went to rehab, which is where he met his new wife, my stepmother. They brought me to his new family, and it was just the beginning of a pivotal point in my life and led to how I would be defined by others and my worth not acknowledged. My dad was a businessman, had his own business as an IT and still trafficked drugs. He was hardly home, always in his office. So, I was left to be in the care of his new wife. It looked perfect on the outside, nice house, luxury vehicles displayed in the yard, we sat in the front row on Sunday, and I went to private Christian school until I was in 8th grade. I participated in cheerleading and track, in school. But looks on the outside are not always what they seem.

Every day I would be walking on eggshells not knowing what mood my stepmother would be in. You see this woman my dad married was emotionally and very physically abusive towards me. Again, another message learned in life by the world that I was not worth protecting, I was not worth being fought for. At a moment in time she had finally got caught after all the years of abuse she had bashed my head until I blacked out and had ringing in my ears. The next day cops came to the school to take me to foster care because her abuse of me had been reported. Did my dad leave her… did my dad fight for me.? No. Another day just left and forgotten, another message I am not important.

The day I went into a foster home was the first day I felt God's peace, I finally felt safe. There were horses on this farm, and this is an important part of my journey, near these horses, was the first time I experienced God's presence, comfort and peace. To this day horses are a huge comfort for me; yet this moment of peace and comfort lasted but a few days.

My mother had found out I was in foster care and wanted to take me out of my one safe place. Side-note she was still active in her addiction, she found my dad made a good amount of money back in the 80's, $600,000 a year was a substantial amount of money, she didn't want me, she wanted the child support. So, I was taken out of my one safe haven into more chaos, drinking, drugs, partying, and more violations of my innocence. My mother would get drunk and tell me she never wanted me, I was a mistake, and because of violations, I was also a slut. These are the words that defined me growing up.

The county caught on to the abuse and at age 15 I was emancipated from my mother. I then went to teen crisis centers, hospitals, lived on the streets. I was making bids on beds at Dorothy Day House so I would have a warm bed to sleep in. I tried getting a hold of my dad through the phone at the shelter, of course my stepmom answered and told me he could not help me; again, he chose her over me. Throughout this timeframe, I felt lost and I had no meaning... I had wanted to die I had many attempts of suicide, but

God kept saving me, I did not know what my purpose was. Of course, through this journey I found someone that told me he loved me, and I fell for it.

19 and now married, I became the victim of domestic violence, my husband brutally beat me for three years, we had a son together. He beat me while I was pregnant and in front of our son, Dante. After he tried taking my life, I divorced him and gave my son up for adoption so he could have the family I never had. The toll it took on my heart to let go of my son so he could have a better life was heavy, to give him a life and family I could not offer. It was the hardest choice I had to make, to know he was safe and had family gave me peace in my heart. Sometimes you have to make sacrifices of the heart for those you love. Those sacrifices can be heartbreaking but necessary, a sacrifice I wish my parents would have done for me.

This indescribable loss was followed by two more abusive relationships. Searching for a love that was never given to me when I myself couldn't define love. One bad choice after another. I kept slipping away into more hopelessness. My private Christian school education planted faith in my heart. I still had that seed of faith and it was fighting inside me to grow and fight to live. It was after the third abusive relationship that I knew I would never settle again and wait on God's best, but before that could happen, I had to heal and love myself.

Over the years, I have had a long season of being single. A season where God has healed my heart. For the first time in my life at age 41

OVERCOMER

I am strong enough to face this head on and face the pain and feelings that come with it. The fear of sharing my story after being silenced for so long, consumed me. But to rise up in boldness and share my story to help give hope is why I finally stood up and wrote.

I thought, nobody wants to hear about the dirt of the family and that is exactly what I was...the dirt. But...during these years of being single I have filled my heart with God, I have let God fill and heal those empty places. He proves over and over again how amazing his love and grace are. He has been my comforter and healer through this all. He gave me strength when I was weak and gave me the boldness to rise up out of the darkness and keep fighting for freedom.

After all that happened to me, I was diagnosed with complex PTSD and this led me to engage in an intensive outpatient program that helped me grow stronger and overcome these memories that haunt my mind. I was very blessed to find a Christian counselor. So, in this season I have absolutely realized that God is my number one focus and everything else will fall into place. He picked up the shattered pieces of my heart, my broken dreams, all of it rebuilt something beautiful. My heart is now full, I'm beginning to let people in, I'm not afraid to love again. My standards have been set high, because for once in my life I love myself and know that I am worthy of love, that in itself was hard to say even a year ago. I believe getting the help you need to get to the root of the issues is absolutely necessary to move forward in this journey we call life. Without counseling and God helping me through, I would still be in a very dark place, stuck in the past with no vision for what is ahead. But through it He has given me amazing healing and fresh vision for what is ahead.

Through this journey of healing I have made some amazing friends and I have finally begun to enjoy life again. I am starting to stand up and speak my story and I pray it gives hope. I now volunteer with human anti-trafficking ministries and I will do whatever it takes to raise awareness and fight for freedom for those still out there. It's time to arise and fight, because if God can help me **overcome**, He can help anyone. He is faithful. When God is not the filling of that void, it can lead to bad choices and relationships.

Most of us that have had past histories similar to this seem to attract these things. Hence it is important to stand on the frontlines and raise awareness for trafficking and to fight for justice. Being a victim of trafficking no longer defines who we are.

Knowing God fills that void is an amazing comfort. When we start filling ourselves with God's truth, these are the fruits:

- ❖ We no longer settle for being treated a certain way.
- ❖ We value who we are.
- ❖ We start dreaming again.
- ❖ We start hoping again.

It took many years to get where I am today. I pray that whoever is reading this right now knows you are worth fighting for and God loves you with an everlasting love. He does not see the mistakes or the stains of your past. You are truly a new creation in him. It is my heart to tell women that you are valuable, you are priceless, his heart beats deeply for you. He loves you with an everlasting love. (Jeremiah 31:3)

His love that is everlasting and what has changed my life. I now live in faith; I spend a lot of time in my word and prayers and have such a huge passion for the voiceless and to give hope to those still feeling hopeless. My journey is far from being over and has had many detours each day, but I keep pushing through, because when I am weak, He is strong. Truly it is because of HIM that I have made it this far. He brought me from the darkest pits into His amazing light with a newfound hope. (Psalms 40)

Please, if you are in a situation you need to get out of, please reach out. I did, and it was the beginning of the rest of my life. God has you in His hands. Step out in faith and let Him guide you. You are never alone in this journey, He will send you people to love and support you, I am living proof of that.

This is only a part of my journey I am sharing with you. I share my story not to gain pity but to show how God can turn our ashes into something beautiful. Because I have been through these things, my relationship with God has been strong, He was my strength, comfort, my peace, my everything through it all. I will rise above all this and have a dream to help others overcome what God has brought me through and out of.

This is how God has changed my thoughts into his truth: To the world I was worthless and unwanted. But to God he sees me as priceless and He adopted me into His family. The king is enthralled by my beauty and He created me for such a time as this, to encourage and give hope to women and to those that have felt abandoned and rejected. I am worth fighting for, He fights on my behalf. I pray my story touches someone's heart and shows you just how big God is. He never leaves us or forsakes us. I pray I can help other women step out in boldness and share their story. If I can touch one person's life and give hope, that will bring so much joy to my heart.

These are the things that pushed me to the frontlines of trafficking to help others get out, show them the love God showed me. All these detours, these rejections, the hurt, the lies, the injustice, they truly pushed me to rise up and fight back. To fight for the injustice of others, to be a voice in boldness. We have a choice in what we do with our wounds, we can either sit in our ash heap and stay stuck or we can rise from the ashes of our past and let it push us forward to the frontlines and keep pressing through. I will not stop fighting for justice and raising awareness. I will continue to work with ministries and do what I can to stand in the frontlines, I pray to one day have my own ministry. But I genuinely believe if we all unite together and become aware and step out in boldness, we can make a difference in someone's life. Together people can make a difference. We are world changers.

We truly are Overcomers. No longer victims but victorious. You have the victory, because if God is for you, who can be against you. Let that be comfort to you knowing He is always there, and He will guide you each step of the way. There is healing, there is hope. Be brave enough to step out in faith and watch God work for you. He can and He will help you through. We are true Esther's of this generation walking in boldness for such a time as this.

Rise up overcomer, you have the victory. Thank you for listening to my story.

About Tiffany Jacobsen

Tiffany Jacobsen is a single mother who grew up in the small town of Medford Wisconsin. She is a first-time author and also public speaker. She has a passion for justice and raising awareness for domestic violence and trafficking as she has personally survived it herself. She is driven to be a voice to a voiceless, to encourage and empower women that have gone through and been through it.

She truly believes that with God and people coming alongside those that are hurting can make a difference in the lives of those that are and have been affected. Her goal is to inspire and give hope to those that are hurting. She has a strong faith in God that she truly lives by, her desire is to be God's heart, hands and feet in the community and be a voice of hope.

She enjoys outdoors and spending time with her son. She uses what she has overcome to encourage others that they can overcome too. She loves to be a light in a dark world. She has a heart to serve. She believes that no matter what you go through, with God on side you can overcome and is truly passionate about making others see the fighter in themselves.

God will always get the glory for the story. Willing to go to the frontlines to fight for justice. Truly believes if each person steps out in boldness in their faith, we can be world changers. Be HIS ♡ heart.

OVERCOMER

Email: <u>Warriorsarise31@gmail.com</u>

Personal web page coming soon.

CHAPTER 2

From Victim to Becoming My Own Hero

By Alejandra Vicent

In 1998, I was just out of high school when I started a relationship that changed my life forever....and I was not even in love.

OK, okay...let me explain.

I have always been the kind of person who is full of life, full of beliefs, full of love.

David was a 5'9", a 200-pound man from Central America with dark eyes. He was 10 years older than me and he intrigued me. We worked together at a restaurant – I was a waitress and he was the bartender. Every night I would sit and wait for one of my parents to pick me up from work and David would keep me company; that is how our relationship started. Sometime later I got my first car and I loved my new-found independence. David and I loved spending time with each other, and we grew close. We would go to his house and listen to John Lennon and drink beer and David would tell me about his life. I was fascinated.

You see, David was always negative, upset, and mad at the world for some reason. He was so miserable all the time. It was so peculiar to me; I did not understand how someone could be in the amazing world we lived in and feel so down all the time. I knew that deep inside he did not want to feel that way and I just *knew* I could help him. And so, David became a challenge for me: I needed to show him how great life could be. I knew how to make the best of the stuff we go through in life and move on. After all, I grew up in a house where my parents had been married for 39 years and were as loving to each other as if they had just met and fallen in love. There were things in my childhood that we went through and that I went through personally (that is a story for another day), but there was love and we were a family. Surely, I could teach him this and help him be happy. I could teach him about my amazing God and how he too could have peace. I could show him the love, respect, and family values with which I was raised. I wanted to bring him into my world of faith, joy, and hope, but, instead, I was pulled into his world of darkness. If only I had known what was to come.

David was a functioning alcoholic but, honestly, it really did not bother me at first. He was actually fun when he was drinking – he would laugh and hug everyone and enjoy himself most of the time. Other times, he would drink and cry and call everyone on his phone to talk about the past. David was raised to be a "macho man" – men are allowed to do whatever they want with no respect for women, who were worthless.

I saw all of this and I could not wait to change him so he could be happy.

The first time I experienced a slap across my face is a day I remember very clearly. David dropped to the floor crying, screaming,

"No, no, no! What have I done? I don't want to be just like my father!"
I dropped onto the floor and joined him. I hugged him and showed
him support, telling him everything was going to be alright.

Shortly after, the slap evolved to him grabbing me and throwing
me across the room and then, to pulling me by my hair and dragging
me all over the house. This went on for years. The triggers were many
and could be ever so small: he might be drunk, he might be
remembering his father's own abusive behavior, or he might have
simply had a bad day and come home to argue with me. Any little
excuse to take it out on me was enough. This became my normal life.
He had hit me, then apologized – use anything in his power to
manipulate me. I got used to my new life.

August 10, 2001, I remember the exact moment my daughter was
born. I could not wait to meet and hold the best gift God was about
to give me. My excitement took a turn, and this is where I had my first
panic attack. The minute I saw her, I panicked. I was suddenly so
afraid, afraid for this new little life – I just wanted to protect her! This
was the moment I realized the life I was leading was broken. My world
turned upside down in that moment and all I could think of was loving
my beautiful daughter and protecting her and giving her the best life
possible.

My parents' example had taught me that a "real marriage" stays
together through good times and bad. After all, I had made the
decision to be with this man, even with all his faults, and I wanted to
show my daughter that she could grow up in a good house, one with

a Mom and Dad at home, a "real" family. So, with that mentality, I took my daughter home and hoped for the best.

My panic attacks increased with time and so did my anxiety. I did not even understand what was happening, but deep inside I knew I was not "crazy." I swore off medication because I was afraid of that making things worse. So, I just did what I always did, I lived with it the best I could and carried on.

Things got worse and life spiraled out of control. I was in such denial.

One day, while we were in the process of moving to a new house, David left his phone on the table and went to pick up more items from the old house. His phone kept ringing and ringing and so I finally answered it. The caller hung up on me. I tried calling back, but they would not pick up and as I listened to the voicemail greeting, I realized I knew this woman. I had never been the jealous type, after all, who would want to be with this monster of a man anyway, but something inside me just *knew* this was his mistress. I did not mention anything to him at first – I was too afraid of him – what if I was wrong? What if I bring it up and give him a reason to beat me yet again? I wrote the number down and started calling it from my phone. Finally, I heard a voice, "Hey, Allie, it's Maria." At this point I was convinced this was an affair, but I wanted to be sure. I took a chance and said, "Hello, Maria, I need you to know that David told me everything and I would like to hear your side of the story." Maria took a big breath and said, "Allie, we have been together for three years. He is a liar and has done nothing but destroy my life. He tells me he loves me and manipulates me into believing him, but I can't do this anymore."

I realized Maria and I were in the same position. I asked Maria to meet me and we drove to my house together to confront David. All I wanted was to confront him and see his reaction when he saw us both walk in together. Sure enough, we walk in and he sees us standing side by side. He looks at us and says, "What, Maria? You know I am with Allie. You know she is the love of my life! So, what are you doing here?" He spoke so matter-of-factly. She left and he simply asked me to drive him to pick up his car from the other house – like nothing was wrong. Of course, I obliged.

As I drove with tears running down my face, thoughts raced through my mind, how many times had I tried to leave? How many times had he threatened me? Threatened to take my daughter, or threatened to kill me? How could I leave here and never come back?

I was so angry and upset that when we got to the house, I had reached my limit. I was boiling mad. I looked him right in the eye and punched him. I punched him as hard as I possibly could. I was terrified, but I was angry. He grabbed his face and congratulated me. He said, "that's right, never take shit from nobody."

And life went back to normal. Our normal.

So normal that even while David's father lived with us for 2 years, he continued to beat me. His father watched this happen over and over and did nothing to defend me or protect me. One day he saw me trying to defend myself and he intervened, but it was just that once. This was my normal.

My panic attacks and anxiety were now coupled with depression. I was getting worse and worse.

A few years later, my daughter, a toddler at the time, looked at me and said, "I don't want my Daddy to hit you anymore." That was the moment I realized that the kind of family I was giving my daughter was worse than being a single mom. I had wanted so badly to give her a "complete family" that I had forgotten we also needed to feel safe and happy.

I prayed and asked God for courage. I grabbed my daughter's clothes and we left. I took refuge in my parent's house where I knew I would always have a home. I was scared and full of anxiety for what was to come, but I had already taken the hardest step and even if the worst thing happened and he killed me, it was something I was sure was going to happen if I stayed anyway. I had nothing left to lose. I knew things might get worse before they got better, but I had hope.

Realizing I was not coming back, my ex became obsessed with me. He would show up at my job and cause trouble for me. One time he came demanding that I turn over the keys to my car, saying it was no longer mine; even though we had purchased it together, the title was in his name and I had no choice but to give it to him. When we walked out into the parking lot, his rage was alive, and he hit me again. I called the police again, as I did after each incident like this, but the only thing that would happen is that I would get a restraining order.

Paper never stopped an assault and so this went on for months and months. He would call me and follow me all the time. I was legitimately afraid for our lives.

Little by little, the calls slowed down and the times he would show up became fewer and farther in between. He was finally getting the message that I was not coming back. I grew stronger.

I stopped taking his calls and I had no contact with him. I set up strong boundaries for myself.

To this day, he continues to attempt to manipulate me through our daughter who is now 18. Through her, he apologizes for everything, begs for forgiveness and I recognize this is the pattern of his instability. But I will never forget all that my daughter and I lived through and I will never go back to that life. Never.

As I grew more stable, I knew I needed to rid myself of the anxiety and panic attacks. I dove into researching panic attacks and gained as much knowledge as I could. I wanted to understand anxiety and to utterly understand the power of the mind, the chemicals in our body and how our minds operate. I dedicated hours and hours and I did it. I overcame my panic attacks and my anxiety.

Today, I am a Life Coach and I help people through experience similar to my own. I teach them that we cannot change the past, but we can definitely change our future. You see, when you become aware, all you need are the tools to help yourself create new patterns and to change your way of seeing things. We all go through hardships in life and maybe you are thinking," My story is worse than hers." I hear you, believe me, there are untold stories from my life that do not fit on these pages that make the one I have shared seem pretty, but I would pose these questions to you:

Do you want to feel differently?

Do you want a different life?

Are you willing to do the work to overcome your past hardships?

I challenge you to do the work and become who you really want to be. Being the victim takes just as much work as being a survivor. When you start seeing your past in a different way, your past will start giving you the power and the courage to become who you truly are. Life will throw stuff your way every day, but you can learn to live a peaceful life knowing that there is nothing you cannot overcome. When you cannot control what is happening, challenge yourself to control the way you respond to what is happening. That is where your power is.

About Alejandra "Allie" Vicent

Alejandra "Allie" Vicent is a Life Coach living and working in Southeast Florida. She immigrated from Venezuela to the United States in 1992 at the age of 12 where she immediately started public school, despite not knowing the English language. Allie adapted and persevered. At 14 she got her first job working as a cashier at a restaurant and spent decades working her way up through the ranks, including several managerial positions. She is known for being dedicated and going above and beyond in all that that she does.

Allie is now working as a Life Coach and is enjoying helping people on a daily basis. She provides the tools needed to change life patterns and live a peaceful, anxiety-free life.

Allie's mission is to help motivate people to take the steps necessary to overcome trauma. She is consistently working on new ideas to assist her clients and move them forward.

After a few failed relationships throughout her life, Allie realized God had her soul mate waiting for her all along. She's joyfully coupled with her dream-come-true life partner who completes her.She has two beautiful daughters, aged 18 and 8, and they are the absolute gifts of her life.

OVERCOMER

Facing Anxiety with Allie

(954)729-7238

facinganxietywithallie@gmail.com

Instagram: alli_life_coach

CHAPTER 3

FROZEN Dawn's Early Light

By Dawn Marie

My father was a violent and sadistic man. He beat my mother viciously and relished in our fear. I watched him pick up the television and throw it at her. I remember the shattered glass. He chased her from room to room while I hid under the bed. I could hear the vile names he called her while she cried and begged for him to stop. These are my earliest memories of feeling utterly powerless and "freezing".

When I was 4 my mother woke me and my older brother in the middle of the night. She said, "We're leaving." I was relieved. We left with just a laundry basket of clothes to a battered women's shelter called "Haven House". Within a few months, we moved to the projects in Sheridan Parkside (Buffalo, NY).

I used to play with a little girl who lived down the street. She had white blonde hair like mine. We looked like sisters. One day she and I wandered to the local corner store and played under some nearby trees. A man pulled up to us and asked if we could help him find a girl named Julie. He asked us to get inside so we could talk about how to find her. My friend sat in the back seat and I sat in the front. Once we got in, there was no more talk of Julie. He drove to a secluded area of the lot. He made me perform a sex act on him. When he finished, he gave me $3.00. My world was shattered in that car, but I pretended everything was okay. He went on to talk about what we would do next time. He asked for our phone numbers. Tammy didn't have a phone, so I gave him mine. He finally let us go. He called often. My mother used to hand me the phone. I sat frozen and listened. His words were sickening.

During these years in the projects, my mother had many men in her life. She was restless, always going out, and coming back with a new guy. She did things with these men right in front of us. One such man was named Scott. He began living with us. He had no job and no patience for kids. He beat me on my 6th birthday, Christmas Eve, I don't remember why. That same winter, my aunt who lived in a nice neighborhood asked my mother to house sit while she went on vacation. We were excited to stay in a nice place for a week. Scott wandered into my room in the middle of the night wearing only a shirt tied at the waist and naked below. I pretended to be asleep, I didn't move a muscle. He opened what I now assume was a jar of Vaseline. To this day I still have flashbacks of this when opening any jar.

The next morning, I told my mother what happened. At first, she didn't believe me. Then she took him down to the basement and confronted him. When she came back up, she was angry with me. He told her he did it because he was tired. There was no other explanation. He continued to stay. These were the coldest, most dreadful and bewildering days of my childhood.

Why didn't she throw him out?

Why didn't she protect me?

I shared what happened with my aunt. She asked, "Why didn't you kick and scream?" I wondered too.

Why didn't I?

Like so many other men in my mother's life, he eventually faded away. That summer, one of the neighborhood guys named "Angel" came to babysit me. He was strange. He didn't talk much. He just stared at me. I fell asleep watching TV in the living room. I woke up to find myself naked with my legs spread apart and him touching me. I froze. I pretended not even to realize I was naked. There was a yellow and white blanket my grandmother had knitted on the couch. I wrapped it around myself and wandered up to my bedroom. Humiliated. Ashamed. I told my mother the next day. She explained he was just changing me and anyway he didn't charge us to babysit. So, it continued. I started begging my friend's mom to let me sleep over. This worked for a time to keep me safe when I knew my mother was going out, but other times I'd have to come home where he would already be waiting for me. I can still remember the smirk on his face.

My mother's older brother Bill often masturbated in front of me. When he did this, again, I froze. I pretended not to notice at all, like it was completely normal. One night he woke me up while I slept on my grandmother's couch and molested me. Here I was again. Why didn't I kick and scream? I told my mother the next day. She didn't believe me. Years later she told me he did the same to her.

OVERCOMER

There were many other men in her life who harmed me. More than I can count. I stopped telling. It never helped.

Around age 7, my mother managed to get a car we called "Hop-Along" because it broke down a lot. She pushed her luck driving it to see her latest boyfriend who was in prison hours away. But while gassing up for the trip, she met the gas station manager. He gave her free gas. She ended up dumping the convict and the gas man became our stepfather. He didn't molest me. He was just miserable and hated us. He beat us bloody or put us through bizarre punishment rituals. Once he tried to choke me. I was 12. When he let go of my neck, I walked out of the house and ended up in a shelter for runaways. I was then placed in a detention center. My mother refused to provide clothes for me, so they put me in an orange jumpsuit reserved for kids who committed crimes. I stayed in a cell with bars on the window, a cot, sink, and toilet. I was treated like a criminal for running away from abuse. As awful as that place was, it was better than going home.

Roughly a year later, my aunt (my father's sister) was given custody of me. She had a nice house. I looked up to her. She encouraged me and made me feel special. We had fun together. I thought everything was finally going to be okay. But things began to change. During my first year staying with her, when I was 14, she accused her husband of fantasizing about me. They had a violent argument. And again, I froze. She beat me for not defending her saying, "Why didn't you stand up for me after all I've done for you?" accompanied by a host of vulgar names. I had no answer. This would be the first of many devastating verbal and physical lashings. Her rage would be triggered if she felt that I loved my biological parents, grandmother or even school friends more than I loved her. Or if she felt she wasn't being glorified enough for "rescuing" me. She often threatened to throw me out on the street for such infractions. I was expected to prop her up, be her best friend and punching bag as needed in exchange for her love and care.

In high school, I found solace in theater, music and reading. I had multiple jobs and spent as little time at home as possible. I auditioned for the American Musical and Dramatic Academy of NYC. I had to sneak and arrange it while my aunt was out of town because she demanded I was to become a nurse just like her and continue to live with her after high school. When my acceptance letter arrived, she raged for days. She broke things. Eventually, she broke me.

I ran away and became an unpaid live-in nanny so I could finish high school. I moved to the Big Apple in the fall to attend AMDA. I was free, technically...but, with that freedom, painful feelings about my experiences started to emerge. I was angry, depressed, anxious, and felt profound loneliness. I had no self-esteem. No boundaries. No judgement.

In spite of this, I graduated, and went on to find success in the modeling and acting industry.

In the 90's in NYC, my agent said I needed new pictures and that he'd arranged a "free" photoshoot for me. That photographer assaulted me. And yet again, I froze. Why didn't I kick him and run out of his studio? It took me 2 days to report it to the police. Months later, I was booked by that same agent to model in a fashion segment on Fox & Friends with two other models. We spent time talking in the dressing room and during commercial breaks. We came to realize we were all assaulted by the same photographer. They never reported it. They didn't want to risk their careers.

After 9/11, I left NYC and began working as a vocalist in South Florida. I also taught acting and modeling classes. I won a handful of "beauty" pageants but also saw how ugly that world could be. I mistakenly thought that a crown and sash would deem me worthy, lovable, and legitimate. Not so.

Shortly thereafter in 2004, I was invited to a middle school Career Day to talk about modeling. I spoke in an open and honest way about how my path was not so glamorous and how I was bullied during my school years. My experiences resonated with the students. Suddenly a roomful of kids opened up about bullying and how it affected them. Hearing their stories set me on a new path. I began speaking at schools on bullying prevention, sharing my history and coping strategies. I later presented school wide assemblies across the country. It felt really good to let these children know they were understood, heard, and that they weren't alone.

In 2014, a cyst on my leg became infected. During a procedure to drain it, my doctor sexually assaulted me. I froze on the operating table. My first call was to my aunt. "Why didn't you kick and scream?" This was just as she had said 35 years earlier...I had no answer...He was later arrested. Eight other women, including his former nurse and patients, came forward detailing similar accounts over many years. The trauma, shame of the event, and stress of going through the legal process caused me to stop my bullying prevention speaking. I also gave up teaching. After all, what qualified me to teach kids to stand up to bullies if the best I could do in the face of abuse was just freeze and not get up off the examining table?

So, I decided that I would just focus on singing. I thought I could hide more easily behind music and not have to directly address my trauma. It didn't take long to fill my calendar. I began singing regularly for then private citizen Donald Trump at Mar-a-Lago as well as many other beautiful establishments in Palm Beach county. My life seemed glamorous and exciting. People didn't know that when I wasn't "performing", there were times when I couldn't leave the house. I closed the blinds and hid in bed. I was afraid of grocery shopping, but it didn't matter because I had no appetite. At one point, I lost 30 lbs. People started asking if I was sick. I was taking three different medications just to sleep. I had horrifying nightmares and panic attacks that left me gasping for air. Sometimes I sat paralyzed for hours before having to go out to sing and appear happy. I thought of checking myself into the hospital. I made out a will. I wrote a letter to my best friend explaining that I had to go, that life was too painful. My dog, Giacomo, was the reason I didn't go through with it. Leaving him alone in the world was an intolerable thought.

I had been in and out of therapy since my early 20's. While it helped to address many aspects of my history, one thing that was left largely unresolved was my pattern of freezing that started as early as I can remember. I watched the #MeToo movement unfold and saw myself through the lens of people who didn't believe the victims who were starting to share their stories. "Why didn't she fight back?". This triggered unbearable feelings of shame.

I needed to understand. I began to research the nervous system. It seems that most people are familiar with the "fight or flight" response to danger. It propels us to act to protect ourselves, but I came to learn that the "freeze" response is just as common, especially in children who are utterly helpless to defend themselves. In a split second, the brain decides that immobility is the only way to survive. Is it really reasonable to expect a small child to fight and escape a grown man? Of course not. I was faced with things so terrifying and so frequently that this primal response became a learned behavior that followed me into adulthood. I wanted desperately to learn how to undo this wiring that no longer served me.

A year ago, I started a new type of therapy I had read about called EMDR (Eye Movement Desensitization Reprocessing). It has allowed me to revisit the most frightening places in my history and rewire my brain's automatic collapse response. I have made great progress, but I have had to let go of the notion that I will achieve perfection. It is a difficult wiring to undo. I celebrate the days I get it right when I am able to speak up and call out predatory behavior right when it happens. Something as simple as looking someone squarely in the eyes and telling him to "Back off" if he is invading my personal space is a victory. I am learning that my boundaries are more valuable than hurting a stranger's feelings.

When I finally let go of the shame I carried for so long, I had so much to share. I returned to public speaking after 5 years. I now teach human trafficking prevention to children and adults. I feel compelled to dispel the myth that victims can "fight" or get up and leave anytime they want. I understand all too well that chains are often invisible. I also educate audiences on "trauma bonding" which is the attachment bond created by repeated abuse by one who masquerades as a caregiver. In sharing these lessons through my own story, I hope to inspire others to free themselves from the prison of the freeze response.

About Dawn Marie

Dawn Marie is also a human trafficking prevention and bullying prevention speaker. She presents at schools, youth shelters, community events, and men's and boy's groups. In 2012 she was honored by the Palm Beach County School District for her countless volunteer hours. Her presentations are dynamic, highly interactive and down-to-earth.

Her efforts have been covered in several local news segments as well as in front-page news in cities across the country. In 2000, she was featured on an episode of Dateline NBC which addressed how attitude and appearance can affect our treatment in society.

To arrange for her to speak at your next event, visit: www.shineassemblies.com.

Dawn has a Facebook group called: **Human Trafficking Heroes of Palm Beach County** where members participate in the planning, execution, and promotion of awareness and fundraising events for human trafficking prevention and resources for providing recovery for victims.

Her music can be found at **www.musicbydawnmarie.com**

CHAPTER 4

Breaking the Chains

By Cynthia Rivera

I am survivor of the sex trade. The experiences of my story are unique to me but the theme around which the details are centered is becoming more widely known. Every year about fifteen thousand (15,000) children are brought to the United States from other countries to be forced into sex trafficking. About five hundred thousand (500,000) children, including children born in the United States will eventually be sexually abused. I can offer you many statistics that lay out the need for therapeutic recovery once girls and women are rescued from their horror of abuse and evil, but I think it is more impactful to put a face to all the anonymous statistics and numbers by sharing my own story.

Let me start tough by giving you hope. What I am about to share of my journey may demand a lot from you. For certain, my telling it demands a lot from me. The story is filled with details of darkness, abuse, and evil but it also includes hope, faith, and healing because I did not die by my abusers' hands or by my own hands. I am here with you.

Before becoming

As a victim of trafficking, I was molested at age seven. It was the first time I knew people had evil intentions. I was washing dishes standing on a white stool so I could reach. I was helping my grandmother since she was taking care of my sister, and at that time my mom was working two jobs to support us and the household. A plumber came and started washing his hands as he stood right behind me. I just froze. I remember not understanding what was going on. He slipped his hand under my dress and started to fondle me. At the time I did not know but I later realized he was masturbating and using a little girl for arousal. I kept this and more… a secret until I was 30.

My next experience came when I was 13. At this time, I was going to my dad's every two weeks. He was never a good man, but I still loved him and thought the world of him despite all of the domestic violence I saw as a child within my home. As usual my father had to go run to his bar, so he dropped me off at his barmaid's place. All I remember was screaming. Yelling "HELP, STOP! HELP! STOP!", but no one heard me in time. I recall running out of the room and throwing up. I could not stop; I could not understand what was happening. I was a virgin and did not realize what happened. It being my father's weekend, I ran to him to tell him I was just raped. Like any daughter I expected love, compassion, and justice but that would not be the case at all. This is the part that was darkest for me. I hugged him and cried and completely lost it expecting that paternal instinct to kick in. What I got was completely different. Then my father turned and slapped me, hard. He called me a whore as I landed on the white daybed, he had bought for me. I was in shock and did not believe what was happening. My father began to rape me. Out of the corner of my eye I saw a stuffed animal. An image symbolic of innocence in childhood staring at us both, while I remained powerless to stop this cruelty. I was sent into foster care after and my real nightmare began with foster mother when she sold me.

Now in the Grips of Trafficking

I could not run because I was in a dark room in the back of a building with two men outside the door. By the sixth month I lost count of how many times I was sold. I tried to stay as numb as possible. I recall a time I asked to go to the bathroom. I started breaking mirrors and cutting myself thinking the mutilation would repulse my rapists. I would try to feel, as my body became foreign to me, nothing, but my mind, heart, and spirit would not let me give up on life.

After a while, the rapes got more often and more violent. At this point I was being sold to cops, attorneys, drug dealers, and famous artists. I have never named them for my own safety, even now I see them on television and I cringe. One of the rapes stands out because it was so violent. It was a cop; an officer of the law sworn to serve and protect. He was gentle at first, then the beating began. I was dragged and thrown against anything and everything in the room. He knew I was a child, but I believe he got off on watching me be scared. At first, every time I saw a cop my PTSD would kick in; flashbacks, nightmares, panic attacks, feelings of terror, they still happen, only more seldomly now.

Why did I not escape?

Why did I not run?

The sex slave owner considered me his personal toy and the rapes got up to 10 to 12 times a day, more aggressive each time. What kind of fight can a 95-pound girl have against a 450-pound brute? I was an easy sell. I was young and inexperienced. Watching me in terror was exciting to them. At one point the rapes were so violent I could not perform due to the pain and ripping. I could not walk. I started to beg one of the bodyguards for help. I could tell this bodyguard had a modest amount of decency and he was disgusted by his boss' actions. Of course, he could not do much because his life would also be on the line. I thank God that the bodyguard spoke to someone and told them what was happening and that I was a child. The cycle of horror continued for a couple of years until a miracle occurred and I was rescued.

The Code of Honor Between Thieves of Innocence

Ironically, even the deviant criminal class maintains a code of ethics. It was this code and respect that turned the tide for me. By means of a more powerful drug lord I was bought from my trafficker. For some mysterious reason he gave me my freedom. He paid so I could live! Once I was rescued and free, I began the hard task of putting myself back together again. This was going to test me further.

Now 28 I thought I was strong, healed, on top of the world. I had just gotten certified to be an x-ray technician and was so proud of myself. I went from x-ray tech to surgical assistant, which was what I wanted to be in order to help others. At this time, I was in Atlanta and had met someone. We got along pretty good, but I got pregnant and decided to have my child. When I made that choice, I knew that sooner or later I would end up a single mother and I was okay with that. When my baby girl was born her father and I were not on the best terms. He had cheated and his ex-wife was poisoned. Around the time my baby was about a month old I was still having trouble moving around due to my c-section. Her father came home from work and I had let his 2 oldest kids play with the neighbors. When he did not see his kids and he realized dinner was not ready, he went into our bedroom and grabbed the gun. He put it to my head and proceeded to beat me with the pistol. Once I fell to the floor he began kicking and continued hitting me with the pistol. All I could do was cover my face. I want to thank God because all I could remember the whole time this was happening was my praying. Asking him, "Please don't let me die, please let me live. I cannot leave my child to be raised by this man". When his sister arrived, she asked him, "What the hell did you do? You have to drop her off at the hospital and I will take the baby. She might not make it!" I just remember waking up at the hospital. I received so many blows to the head that my optic nerve is now very thin. If I receive another hard hit to my right side my optic nerve could detach, and I could go blind. I waited a month before I returned home. My face was deformed from the beating and that would have given my mother a heart attack.

When I got home, I began healing and loving myself, knowing this was not my fault. It took me a long time to love myself and know my value and my strength. Every morning I would tell myself in the mirror, "You Cynthia are a warrior. My spirit will see me through this." I started group therapy and that was a blessing. I learned so much and was healing correctly. Years ago, I started speaking in public, sharing my story, and helping in the rescue of other victims. I was bringing them home safe, getting them the help, they needed. This became my positive outlet. I have always believed in the idea of taking a negative and turning it into a positive. All the hell I went through, I used it to help others who had been through the same. I started with my community. Parents that did not trust the police would come and ask me for help. I now know it was God with me every time, hearing my prayers for these kids and their parents.

I Couldn't Be Wiped Out

Then my friend and I started a nonprofit, **Project Giving Back Houston**, with the Mayors Juvenile Task Force. The program was 100 percent a success. The help these kids need is immense, and what the force does for the kids that no one wants to help is praiseworthy and amazing of them. I am an Advocate for our city but help and support District H and District J.

District J has the highest sex trafficking numbers in Houston and works with domestic violence victims. I have facilitated and taught alongside other advocates, workshops on Human Trafficking in Houston community centers. One program very dear to my heart, Letty's Promise allows students to learn about bullying, sex trafficking, LGBTQ issues, date rape, and mental awareness, and it is now in some

HISD schools. For over 8 years now I have been helping and serving in nonprofit organizations.

Some stories are hard to swallow. They can leave sadness within. One rescue was a bit scary. A girl took off with a gang member. He was over 18, she was 14. Her mom called me crying and headed to my home. I was already looking for her. When mom showed up at my door, I had to catch her because she fell to the ground. She was crying and saying that she could not find her daughter. This parent did not speak English. Again, the grace of God helped me find her. I found out the gang that had her and I shook my head. I knew the head leader of the gang from when I was in middle school. I reached him and in a nice voice said, "I want the girl back or else." I told him he had two choices, drop the girl off anywhere public within 30 minutes or I would have every Gang Task Force in his hood breaking down doors to find her. His people were not clean, they were drug dealers. It would mess up his business over a 14-year-old girl one of his soldiers had. I told him I did not think it was worth it. I encouraged him to bring her back before it cost him his operation. Twenty-five minutes later she was dropped off at a grocery store and I took her home. I sat her down with her mom and explained what that gang member was going to do to her.

When I hear these stories, is when I hit the gym harder, I run, I journal. Self-compassion has power. I gave myself that and it helped me with shame, reducing nightmares, and understanding that none of what happened to me was my fault. I surround myself with women who are wholehearted; those who give back to the less fortunate, to our youth, and to other women. I am a Leader of my community, I am a survivor, I am a success, and I am an overcomer.

I shared my story so you know that it does not matter what your past is. It does not define who you are, the actions you take now do.

My biggest help and savior is God, who has given me the voice to speak so that someone can read it and say that is me, and if she can be a success so can I. Do not get me wrong I have some days that are not so good, and I have amazing days. PTSD is very real and hard to direct to a positive outlet. My outlets are public speaking, helping our youth, helping women who are involved in domestic violence.

I have been the head of management at a company with over 10 years of experience training and supervising production staff, while planning and implementing sales strategies. I work closely with senior management. I am a board member of the Chamber of Commerce, a board member of Baker Ripley Community Centers, and I am immensely proud to be a board member of the Mayor's Hispanic Advisory Board. I am a passionate community leader and servant. I make positive changes in communities and take pride engaging in a civically based approach to community building. My accomplishments are why I believe you can make it also. You can overcome anything and everything you are going through or have gone through.

If I could overcome all of this and become who I am, so can you.

About Cynthia Rivera

Cynthia Rivera has been the head of Management at Alamo Tamales Co. with over 10 years of experience training and supervising production staff, while planning and implementing sales strategies. Cynthia works closely with senior management to implement strategic goals for marketing and sales activities within the budget and timeframes. She is also responsible for creating leads and following them.

A passionate community leader, she has made a positive change in communities and individuals through advocacy empowered by compassion. She takes pride engaging in a civically based approach to community building.

Cynthia is an advocate for District H and J working with sex trafficking and domestic violence victims. She has implemented human trafficking workshops in Houston community centers. Letty's Promise being one very dear to her heart is now at some H.I.S.D schools; which allows students to learn about issues like bullying, sex trafficking, LGBTQ, date rape and mental awareness'. For a few years now, she has been working with Mayors Anti-Gang Juvenile Force in Project Giving Back, she will continue to educate and advocate our youth.

She is also active in non-profit organizations like Home of Hope to develop new programs for at risk youth and mentoring the counselors. She is a board member of Northside Chamber of Commerce, Baker Ripley Centers, and Mayors Hispanic Advisory Board and also part of the Mayors Events subcommittee and Arts subcommittee. She is the voice of those that don't have one in her community.

CHAPTER 5

Chosen

By: Dr. Jessica Vera

It has often been asked, Dr. J., "Why did you answer this call? Why did you choose to become a voice for the voiceless, a frontline Warrior for the movement to end human sexual exploitation and trafficking?" The response I now give is, "I'm chosen, and I've now surrendered, and I am abiding."

I do not believe in coincidences, but I do believe in fate or more specifically in an ordained path that was predesigned in detail for each of us before we even came into existence by our Creator. I know from my own experiences over the last five decades that we will struggle with this truth, because by design we have free will. We will choose to avoid rather than to abide.

It can look something like this, as a young girl I thought of things from that perspective. Everything that I had been taught up until that point had been driven by pain. Pain that I did not inflict on myself nor seek, but rather pain that was caused by objectification by others, as a sexual being at an incredibly young age. Pain of living through early dissension in my home because of marital discord, the challenges of a blended family and the lack of abiding to a core connection to the Creator.

OVERCOMER

Pain is universal, we have all experienced it. Pain is an influential teacher that can skew perceptions and that teaches us to navigate the world from a broken lens. Early experiences can and do leave residues that cloud our judgement and impact our decisions. It can take a lifetime to eliminate, particularly if pain is compounded over years. That is if and only if, you take it upon yourself alone to refine, restore... The absolute I have come to learn and understand is that only God can redeem you to all that you were and are intended to be.

I am trained in human sciences and philosophy therefore what I am sharing in realms of the world is contradictive to what is believed of humanity, from proven study, as truth. After 25 plus years of examining philosophy and empirical research, as well as working with the psyche and behaviors of others and systems, at their worst circumstance, I know that I can inspire others to be their best. This is a wonderful gift. But in order to be redeemed there has to be more than inspiration spoken or read into our lives, we have to act, and this requires faith.

Those early years were rough and as I reflect and mature one thing is certain, the experiences taught me so much more than I had once thought. Through pain I realized achievement. Through pain I realized relationships. Through pain I realized some of my greatest lessons and experienced some of my greatest worldly successes. I know you are probably thinking but why through pain. I wish I had that answer. All I can share is that it is because of the specific pain I experienced that today my gifting through developed resiliency of survivorship has led me to refine as a servant-leader, to be empathetic and compassionate, relatable, an active listener and extremely grateful. This was not accomplished in my own will, but by God. There is nothing impossible with God.

However, without Him, I wandered the world seeking approval, recognition, applause, and affection -- Value from man. I stored up riches, an alphabet soup of initials behind my name, and chased the aloof "Dragon", as I like to call it. The unattainable, never satisfied the need for more.

Do not misunderstand me, I am not minimizing worldly accomplishments or the meaning they can give, but these are fleeting without God. You see we are promised riches beyond imagination, peace without understanding, and the grace of unconditional love, we cannot earn, with God. When we abide by His absolutes, we become unapologetically wise.

If you were given the choice what would you choose material possession or wisdom?

If you asked me this question in my moments of vulnerability, I would answer, "Both." It is a struggle. One that I am challenged with at times primarily when I buy into the overarching cultural paradigm that is a mix of me-centeredness [hedonism] and social relativism. The first purports that "I" is most important before others, and that I need to avoid pain and move towards pleasure. The latter simply is that truth is what the truth is believed to be by the person who sees and thinks it.

OVERCOMER

These cultural influences of today, were recently tested by a global pandemic, Covid-19. This virus that some suspect rightfully so was man-made, reaped havoc on life as we had all known it till now. The silver lining that I have seen, because that is just how I am wired, has been a return for some to the basics. Spending more time with loved ones. Enjoying simple things like observing nature, taking walks, slowing down. An increased appreciation for the things taken for granted previously. Or for others, who thrive in chaos, it has been a time to reinvent themselves, to stay busy taking advantage of every opportunity and to create anew. No judgement, there is no right or wrong way to manage crisis. What has been most important to me as an observer, has been seeing how the global pandemic has set the world on pause first and then on a reset. My prayer is that the reset leads us all back to our Creator.

To every silver lining, there is the backside. In my world in this season, it is the human trafficking criminal enterprise that steals freedom for profit. During the same timeframe that many were living their best through crisis, monsters [predators] were lurking in plain sight preying on our children and the marginalized in our communities. It takes a unique set of lenses to really see the evil that is so awfully close. These lenses were gained through painful experiences. But now they provide 20/20 vision. The subtleties of coercion and frailties of those, who these predators seek to steal, are insidious. To the naked eye they go unnoticed, but for those **chosen** the clues from the patterns are obvious.

I am not going to lie there are days, even now that I wish that I could live in denial to the hideous reality that so many, including myself experience to some degree in life. It has been my professional experience that every mental block and physical systemic ailment is a derivative of past unresolved abuse, neglect, or exploitation and that in a large percentage of cases the aftermath experiences lead to influence in every aspect of human functioning. A pretty bleak conclusion if this were the end, but it is not, I have also witnessed and experienced how we can lay down our burdens, release our sufferance [forgive] and be redeemed.

We are intricately woven, there was no detail left to chance. A masterpiece in the Creator's hand that is a work in progress. When you hear, see, or feel the Call, it is difficult to ignore. Even when you have tried every way to avoid it and believe me when I tell you, I have, it pursues you relentlessly. Let me share a secret, we are all Called.

We are all chosen, set apart.

Why did you answer the Call Dr. J.?

The Call, resonated at the core of my being, as I could not allow us to lose one more soul to the grips of evil. The images that resurfaced were vivid reminders of that once little girl in the corner of her bed, or a sofa, or a room, shaking, pretending to be asleep, not moving a muscle, unable to make a sound, even though inside she was screaming at the top octave of her voice. Or of the young high-powered, successful lady, who at the top of her business game, was raped repeatedly, without a second thought for the word "No." And images of the multitude of girls and boys whose faces will forever be imprinted in my mind's eye, while serving in juvenile detentions, the dependency system and as a mom of a teenager. This had to be stopped.

But how?

Sexual immorality and greed have been roots of evil since the beginning of time. Initially these thoughts were overwhelming. Until it became crystal clear that I was chosen for this work and that our Creator equips the unequipped and that it would not be Jessica against the evil in the world, but a tribe of Warriors pushing back the darkness, by shining our Light, as an unextinguishable beacon of hope.

But God.

Even as I write the words on these pages it is unbelievable to me how everything that was created to destroy and to cheat me of life has been redeemed to wholeness. In answering the Call and in acceptance of being chosen brought with it a wave of wisdom and peace that is difficult to explain. Although many times, my mind tries to tell me that things are not possible, I take those thoughts captive and what I hear instead is everything is possible with expectant confidence in God. By abiding, the whisper impresses, *"Do not lean on your own understanding rather lean into faith and an unwavering hope that comes only from being connected to Me."*

How does abiding look in daily life?

If you ask my friend, family, or colleagues, they might answer with words like, "Unrelenting workaholic, multitasker, overachiever, ambitious, bold…" I know this because I have asked, and the people I surround myself with keep me accountable and share their truth of me with me in authenticity. During a recent Mother's Day, my precious daughters shared their perceptions of their mother with words such as, "Example of success, encourager, selfless, a kick-ass hard worker, who does not give up." What I did not hear was a follower of Christ. This left me with a sense of urgency to take inventory and to reset, realign and reconcile my core with my Creator. Abiding is a lifesaving process; it is not something you do once and then magically it becomes ingrained in your essence. It requires daily connection with absolute Truth, maturation of the spirit by practicing love, joy, peace, patience, kindness, goodness, faithfulness, gentleness, and self-control. It also means release of the fleeting wants of the world.

I know…abiding at its simplest means remaining connected to the source of life at all times, even when it is not convenient. Even when for example, you want to default to ways of being that have proven successful in attaining things or achieving accolades. For me it has meant establishing and building a Nonprofit Nongovernmental Organization to **End Lost Innocence To Exploitation (ELITE) Foundation** currently dependent on volunteerism. I did not grow up in the USA and knew nothing about building a nonprofit company. As I shared, I had early success in building multimillion-dollar for-profit organizations. But the nonprofit world is different.

OVERCOMER

Here is a snapshot of the view of nonprofits from the top. According to Dan Pallotta, "What we have been taught to think about giving and about charity and about the nonprofit sector, are actually undermining the causes we love, and our profound yearning to change the world...Philanthropy is the market for love...Yet, although social problems are massive in scale, our nonprofit organizations are tiny up against them, and we have a belief system that keeps them tiny. We have two rulebooks. We have one for the nonprofit sector, and one for the rest of the economic world.

"It is an apartheid, and it discriminates against the nonprofit sector in five different areas:

1. Compensation [over 25% spend on admin operations is consider appalling].

2. Resources spent on advertising and marketing. Giving remains stuck at two percent of GDP, ever since we started measuring it in the 1970's. That is an important fact, because it tells us that in 40 years, the nonprofit sector has not been able to wrestle any market share away from the for-profit sector.

3. Taking of risk in pursuit of new ideas for generating revenue [frowned upon].

4. Time [nonprofits have to produce a return to the cause immediately] and

5. The nonprofit sector is starved for growth and risk and idea capital.

See the dilemma. There was no coincidence that the nonprofit landscape is primed ready to be changed. Here too my life's entrepreneurial experiences could be leveraged to equip for the Call. Human trafficking is the purest example of the evil of greed. Each person who is objectified as a commodity is sold and bought at a higher price the younger and purer they are. The average usage of a human being for the sex trade has been estimated at 10-12 rapes daily or a potential of 25,550 rapes across the estimated lifespan of a victim [7 years].

What is the value of a life?

Priceless.

Yet, the supply and demand of human beings for the sex trade is estimated to be big business earning upwards of $200,000,000 annually. There is a need for significant disruption to this pipeline, to end stolen freedom for profit. This will entail a radical shift in the prospectus of nonprofits. There is a need to build a tribe of abiding Warriors with unwavering faith and hope, as well as expectant confidence because despite the goliath of his criminal enterprise, it can and will be knocked down by a simple stone between the eyes, ordained by God.

I am chosen, and I have now surrendered, and I am abiding, how about you?

OVERCOMER

Reflect and Respond:

_____

_____

_____

_____

The Call, when you answer it, it provides direction to your purpose and purpose to your passion. You were created for this time specifically. There is nothing that you cannot do with God because there is nothing impossible for God.

Believe. Abide. Be Set Free.

About Dr. Jessica Vera

Dr. J., a writer, entrepreneur, philanthropist, and an unwavering visionary, believes in YOU. Her platform from trauma to servant-leader, is built from experience of compound pain, creating several successful international for-profit companies; and a nonprofit flagship, Elite Foundation (headquarters in Florida).

Elite Foundation creates a safe haven for all who have suffered trauma from vulnerability to human exploitation in all its ugly forms. Elite's Vision is to co-create a future for every Survivor. Through Elite's three silos of goods and services the Foundation fulfills its mission to educate, empower and to transform lives.

Dr. J. and Elite Foundation currently lock-shields with Warriors, who share the belief that the greatest gift of success in life is reciprocity. To Dr. J., success is measured not by what one accumulates in this lifetime; but by the souls we have the privilege to positively impact. She is a fervent believer in the power of prayer, has an unwavering adoration for her Creator and the Love that she has been shown and has the privilege to share with others willing to receive it.

Dr. J.'s personal vision is to empower 1,000,000 souls to live out their full potential in life and business, through socially-conscious business practices that fund freedom. She participates in her community by speaking, teaching, and serving. As a licensed, post-doctorate trained Transformational Practitioner, she has helped thousands of individuals and systems to transform to actualize potential.

Happily married for 20 years+, with two beautiful daughters, Dr. J. strives to intentionally live out a balance of love, life & work.

To learn more about Dr. Jessica Vera please visit **www.drjvera.com**

To learn more about Elite Foundation please visit **www.EliteFundsFreedom.org**

PART II

The Realization to

Be Free

CHAPTER 6

Five Steps to Go from Fearful to Fearless

By Wendy Elliott

While growing up, I remember a little girl that I thought was the luckiest in the world. She was happy go lucky, she was beautiful, she had loving parents, family, and friends. Nothing appeared to daunt her, her life was pretty perfect.

Even in the midst of losing a parent she appeared to still be happy and loved. After a brief life adjustment, her life continued to show excitement, fun and achievements as she grew up. Although she lived in a small town with little to do, she was always finding ways to keep herself active and involved in pretty much everything there was to do. She appeared so confident, a natural leader in her Sunday school class, in her school classroom and in her extracurricular activities. She had so many friends and was always leading them into what she felt was "greatness" whether it was to build a cabin in the woods, making a grape vine swing or as the captain of the cheer squad, majorette team and 1st chair of trumpet in the band. Nothing could hold her back.

She continued to be successful throughout her grade school time and even transferred to another school to be in the high school band. So bright that the school asked her mom to go ahead and allow her to go directly to high school. Fortunately, her mom declined because she wanted her to have the social maturity that came with spending time with her peers. This did not stop her, she continued to excel academically, musically and continued to build her social circle leading the challenge in all she did. She so enjoyed the challenge in learning new things. Nothing daunted her, she was a sponge, she wanted to know it all and achieve it all. Life and her future were amazing!! She appeared so confident in who she was, what she was capable of doing and how she was going to accomplish it **ALL!!**

Then something changed her Freshman year of High School. She met an amazing young man that she knew was going to be the love of her life. He was going to complete her, to make her even better. His influence and drive appeared to be just as passionate as hers. They were going to be so happy, so much would be accomplished, they were as one.

One problem!!

He was a Senior and would only be there for one more year before he went to college. That was ok, he had already figured it all out, the school he chose was just a few hours away and he would be home every weekend. Then when she graduated, she would join him there, at the college he chose. What an awesome plan! The one year they had together was great, they spent almost every day endlessly planning their future.

Three years went by, she was engaged, still active in school actives, leading with challenges, but it appeared the light had faded, the excitement was shaded there was hesitation in all she did, there was almost a fear of some sorts. Yes, she did skip her Junior year of high school and now was in with students that she barely knew, but there was something else. She often sat in the corner of the room not talking with others, particularly boys in her class, she would walk by herself instead of the crowd around her, she rarely even spoke with her girlfriends of years. Something had changed inside of her. Her confidence in her skills and ability had faltered as though she had gone through a huge defeat. Others wondered what had happened, and when asked she would just turn on her charm and indicate she was just anxious about going to college next year and focusing on what she wanted to do there.

Finally, graduation time!!! She was excited to finally get to be with her fiancé and go to college however the one he went to did not have the degree she wanted to pursue. He assured her that she was really talented in other areas and all would be fine. Hesitantly she struggled to find her calling. This was the best plan of course as they were meant to be. How amazing someone loved her that much to just take care of everything for her. It appeared as though her confidence was floundering, but he was there to support.

It was time to start, she again was going to try out for the band, choir and of course wanted to be the "twirler" since they did not have a majorette team. She prepared all summer and **GOT IT all!!** Again, her spirits were high, she did it, she was proud once again of her accomplishments and was ready for her future. Her fiancé was excited too. He always encouraged her to look her best, make sure she did not eat too much so she would always look good, how sweet of him to always be thinking of her. However, she was concerned and felt that she needed to be better, look better and of course she obviously had not accomplished that.

Interactions with her fiancé started to become uncomfortable, they started to focus on how she needed to behave, to look and what he thought her future would be like. She reluctantly followed the rules set forth. She was so grateful for him taking such good care of her, she could not imagine life without him. She had never had anyone that cared for her this much, no one that ever helped her make decisions that were in her best interest keeping her safe from things that may be hurtful and harmful. She would lay in bed at night in her dorm and cry to God to make sure he kept him safe as she did not know what she would do without him. She was so fortunate!! Her life was amazing.

But was it?

Well if you have not figured it out by now!!! This was me. This bright, active, confident, nothing can hold her back, young lady that managed to convert to someone that was totally opposite!! Someone that was dependent on someone else to make her life whole! I went from bold and Fearless to Fearful of almost everything in life unless I had someone that I thought loved and adored me in my life giving me permission, telling me how to do it. Pleasing others had become my life, taking care of myself was not a part of that. *Who was this? What happened to the young lady that had all the confidence in the world and could conquer it all?*

OVERCOMER

We may have all had relationships that we thought were perfect and come to find out they were the most harmful and impactful in our lives even if it is us having the bad relationship with ourselves. We cannot allow that one instance to be the overarching story of our being. However, we often self-sabotage by allowing those feelings of self-doubt, of worthlessness and **FEAR** to come to the forefront.

What can we do about that?

TONS!!!

We may not be cognizant of that; however, we just have to shift our mindset to be **FEARLESS**.

For decades I was plagued by the bully in my head. She told me I was weak, I was unworthy, I did not know what I was doing and that I needed validation from others to move forward. Thankfully, I figured out that she was a liar, I moved on from that relationship looking for a better person to run my life…**ME!!**

Do not get me wrong, in the grand scheme of things my life has been nothing but wonderful, I look at it as having many seasons of growth, of failures and of successes that I always can and will learn through.

What I have come to realize however, is that the relationship experience described in my story was probably the most impactful as it seemed to have propelled me personally into a person that was in constant doubt of her self-worth, of her ability to do things well and needing validation that it was an accomplishment. This impacted my personal life, but not my professional life where I was confident, almost an overachiever of sorts.

Personally, I had constant feelings that I was not worth it, I did not deserve to be happy. Fear's a funny thing. It motivates us to hold onto things and people that are not good for us, just because those things and people are less scary than the unknown. On the other hand, I was having a wonderful career that has continued to propel me forward, making me feel like I am a success and not always failing. A segmentation of sorts. My career has always been my solstice, it has always been my liberator from being overwhelmed with personal and relational turmoil. I had to find out why my relationships were not in sync with my career.

Could I not have both?

Could I not be satisfied in my work and my relationships?

FEAR was the monster in my mind, in my confidence, in my being. I was fearful. Fear was happening not only in my relationships but in me....I was fearful of what I was to become, how to become what I wanted and how to do things that were not in my comfort zone. I had to make sure I cared about myself as I had cared about others throughout my life.

I needed to tackle **FEAR,** it was time for me to take risks, to be bold and to fail forward. It was time for me to be **FEARLESS**. How was it that when I was at my corporate job, I had no problems coming up with ways to tackle challenges and make changes occur, yet in my personal life I was so unsure of myself, I was afraid to step outside of my comfort zone? That just did not make sense to me. I had to figure this out. It had taken so many years from me, years that I could have done so many other things.

FEAR!!!!

FEAR: False Evidence Appearing Real

**I had to do a complete Mindshift and add the other half

LESS: Leveling Everything thru Success Strategies.

I knew what I had to do. As with other things in my life, I had to approach **FEAR** the same way as I had tackled work projects, I have an MBA, I know how to take things on and come up with a plan to accomplish how to make it happen. I have always been successful in tackling the hardest projects and problems as long as I had a plan to do it. It was not always easy and there were always unexpected setbacks, so I had to alter the trajectory of the plan, but I still had a plan.

My mantra has always been to "**Plan the work and Work the Plan.**" Why had I not thought of this before? I had to approach **FEAR** from a position of power, not of helplessness. I was giving my **FEAR** way too much power. It was limiting my mind; it was holding me back from loving myself and all that I am truly capable of doing.

I had attended tons of self-help, vision-board building, claim your power conferences, but they just did not resonate. They all made me feel powerful....for a bit, then I just got confused as to the steps to take to make it all happen. But this I could sink my teeth into.

I jumped right in! I started out by completing a **SWOT** analysis (strengths, weaknesses, opportunities and treats) of my current situation, then stood back and reviewed all of those items, then began to tackle my **goals and objectives** as to where I wanted to grow.

Oh wow, this was so releasing...I was actually seeing how the road map to being **FEARLESS** was coming about. I was seeing light at the end of the tunnel. This may actually work! I needed to look at all the things that I needed to succeed in. Not just overcoming the fear of self-worth but tackling all of my roadblocks that I attack myself about each day. How do I look, how do I dress, how do I get the relationship I deserve and desire? If I wanted to change, **I had to change**, I cannot ask others to do so. I have to "**Just do it**"...(Borrowing from Nike).

After I identified where I stood, I set out to do a **Mission and Vision** statement of my life. What was it I hoped to accomplish and what would that look like? This was great, why had I not thought of this before.

Now it all makes sense to me, this was the language that made me successful as a businesswoman, now I was confident it would be the answer to making my relationship with myself the same! The rest just flowed. Not perfectly, there were a lot of blocks as to how to make things work, but I was kind and realistic with myself knowing that I could always amend and review the plan I was devising.

OVERCOMER

The next steps were creating a **business plan** with specific objectives and goals, identifying those strategic objectives that I wanted to work on for the next 3-5 years and then of course the **deployment plan** as to how I was going to make it work. There it was.... I had my life plan to accomplish not just self-love and worth, but to be able to **Overcome** all my fears and doubts. How to go from **FEARFUL to FEARLESS**!!

If you want something different you have to do things differently. The old verbiage that the definition of insanity is when you do the same thing over and over again, expecting different results, is so true. There is no way around it, you have to make a difference in how you respond and change the result by changing the path. Some days it seems like there is a lot to be scared of. But trapping yourself in a fear spiral will not help you, or the people whose lives your light can help transform. They need you more than ever!

I never want to look back 10 years from now and think " *I am so glad I settled and never truly found my freedom from* **FEAR.**" *I want to embrace what I am* **FEARFUL** *of and step into the* **Overcoming Influencer** *I know I am"*. It always helps me to remember that people are counting on me to show up. When I think of THEM instead of focusing on my own fear, I am able to step past the fear and let my light shine.

I am not suggesting everyone will relate to the business plan method to remove their fears, but for me it was what I needed to be able to tackle the very thing that was holding me back, the thing that made me hate myself for not being better, for not changing things as they continued to happen. It is my language. It's how I see the world of helping myself.

We all have to work through where we are and where we want to be. It is hard and not comfortable and for me it will always be a plan in motion, as I am not where I know I can be or want to be. I struggle every day and forget what I want and begin to doubt myself and my skills to do what I know I need to do to be the best I can be. But now I have my plan, I have my roadmap to success. I just need to follow that and never look back to regret what I have not done. The best part of it is that I have the ability to share this with others that look to me for strength and leadership not just for my business and corporate skill but for being the best I am.

By being on **OVERCOMER.**

Oh, by the way, for that Bully that comes at me every so often, I just tell her to check out my deployment plan **item #1** where she is **"kicked to the curb"!!!!**

5 steps to overcome the fear of worthiness and be successful

1. Analyze your current situation SWOT

2. Develop your Mission and Vision of who you are and what you want Visualize your success and list your Outcomes

3. Decide and Plan your short and long-term path to success

4. Develop a checklist of what you are going to do and how you will accomplish it

5. Enjoy the **Journey** instead of **Obsessing** over the **End Result,** Check your progress regularly. Take consistent action until the accomplishments of your goals are realized!

About Wendy Elliott

Wendy Elliott, MBA/HCM; MA-CCC-SP is a true believer that you can be on the corporate ladder as well as have an entrepreneurial spirit. Wendy began her career as a healthcare provider and rapidly moved up into the leadership roles in somewhat often unique venues always having that entrepreneurial view of things. Wendy has multiple advanced degrees and over two decades of experience in neuroscience, behavioral health and healthcare management, executive corporate development and startup businesses.

Although, Wendy began her career as a healthcare provider she rapidly moved up into leadership roles where she combines her unique expertise in advanced neurosciences, complex adaptive systems approach and business acumen to design an innovative behavioral methodology to helping team members, leaders and providers to overcome many obstacles in order to impact immediate, meaningful and permanent change. Wendy is a true believer that you can be on the corporate ladder, as well as have an entrepreneurial spirit. Wendy empowers others to, **"Plan the work and work the plan,"** to overcome all obstacles and obtain one's passion-driven goals.

Wendy's goal is to take what she has learned throughout her career and coach/teach others how to use their exceptional talents and God given gifts to get what they want out of life. Wendy is a multiple bestselling author and publisher, John Maxwell success coach, Genotype Life Coach, Lifework Leadership graduate and mentor-leader. She is the co-founder of **Elite Foundation** and the Founder/CEO of **Business Lynx, LLC**

You can reach her on **Facebook**, **LinkedIn**, and **Instagram**

To learn more about Elite Foundation please visit **EliteFundsFreedom.org**

CHAPTER 7

A MOMENT ALONE TO GRIEVE

By Pangeline Edwards

The windows shook as the wind howled. I could hear the rain pit-pit-pitting against the glass panes. Someone laughed. A motorcycle raced by. The roaring of its engine broke the noise of the storm, just for a moment. Alberto was not going to be outdone. It was his time. He was here to make an impact. Subtropical Storm Alberto, the first named storm of the 2018 Atlantic hurricane season, howled in to remind me that man can plan, but God is still in control. You may think you can predict the weather, but just like life, you really cannot foresee what is waiting up ahead.

Inside, another storm was raging. I tossed and turned on my bed as the clock struck 2 a.m. I didn't want to get up again, but the urge to pee was great. I flung the sheet off me and jumped out of the bed onto the cold floor. With eyes closed, I moved into the bathroom and did what I needed to do. I always kept my eyes closed because I didn't want to interrupt my brain with light. I want sleep not a mind racing with thoughts and "what ifs".

When would they stop?

When would my nights of no sleep end?

OVERCOMER

Why couldn't I be like normal people who, as soon as their head hit the pillow, were fast asleep?

I have a friend who, no amount of noise, or light, or storm could wake her from her blissful, peaceful sleep. How I wish I were her right now.

I returned to the bed wishing, but now uncomfortable. Hot from all the movement, here it came. Hot flash! Night sweat! Menopause! Call it whatever you like, the effect is the same. Heat rushes to the skin and then the sweat covering my face, my neck, moving down, spreading until my entire body is covered with a slick film of moisture. There was no point in trying to wipe it away. Any more movement would just worsen it.

I laid down or should I say threw myself down on the bed. My head hit the pillow and the white cotton hand towel that laid there. A clean one put there each night to roll my face in and wipe the sweat. This, and my feather pillow, gives me some relief. But only for a few minutes because next comes the chills and the goosebumps as my body tries to regulate itself. I bet you didn't know that cold chills cause just as much discomfort as hot sweats. Menopause madness!

When wills this end?

I closed my eyes. The storm outside raged on.

I don't know which was stronger, Tropical Storm Alberto or the storm that was playing out in my head and more than that, in my heart.

Sometime during the night, I must have fallen back to sleep. I know that because the sounds of the storm were no longer playing outside. Instead, the gentle daylight peeking through the blinds, nudging me to get up, this made it clear that I had slept.

I didn't want to get up. I just wanted to sleep and forget about the insistent conversations taking place in my head, but it was too late now. The storm had passed and the voice that came loud and clear said, "*It's time.*"

I sat up, not sluggish and unwilling as I did most mornings. This time I was wide awake, with a purpose. Today, if it took every ounce of energy from me, I had to get the conversations out of my head and the only way I could do that was to write them down. It was now or never. I had to remove the stage from in my head and put it on the clean, white pages of a Word document. If I was going to move into the next chapter of my life with my sanity intact, I had to tell the story.

Was it my story or Pearline's story, I was not sure? Of course, I am sure. It is her story as it was lived through my eyes. Her story is my story and it needs to be told. If not, I will never have any peace, and sleep will not come, and the storms inside my head will rage long after the storms outside have passed.

I walked into the living room, crossed to my desk, and turned on my laptop. While I was in the bathroom performing my morning rituals, it too went through its optimizing, synching, and refreshing. I went in the kitchen and turned on the coffeepot. I would need a big mug, black and strong, for what I was about to do. Today, there would be no more excuses. There would be no time for procrastination. Today, it was one hundred percent serious business. No more writer's block. That stopped now. It was time.

Loss!

One minute you are on top of the world, pleased with your accomplishments, focusing on the next goal, and suddenly, without a moment' s notice, you are facing a big problem that takes away every ounce of your strength. Mentally, physically, emotionally, and spiritually you are beaten up. Some of you had an idea it was coming, but you did not expect it would be so devastating. The majority of you did not.

Your job gone with no recourse. Your home destroyed. Your health attacked by sickness or disease. Your loved one taken from you. Major life changing ordeals that leave you at a loss. You do not comprehend it so for now you try to function the best you can, but really you cannot. You need help. You need it now, but from where or from whom.

It was not until a few days after my mother's funeral that it hit me. A tsunami of emotions one after the other. I was sad, painfully sad. Mom was gone. The woman who was my mother and friend, both a blessing and a headache, was laid to rest eternally. I was relieved. She was no longer suffering. No more pain and discomfort. Now she had no reason to be frustrated because she could not control the situation. I was angry. Boy was I angry. Her life was over and that made me angry for so many reasons. I was angry with myself, with her, and with God. I was miserable. I felt lonely, isolated, and helpless. I was lost.

Grief is real, very real. Just like fear, grief plays havoc on our emotions because there are so many conflicting feelings taking place within us as we grapple to understand what is happening or has happened. Grief is a normal and natural reaction when someone or something important to you dies or tremendous change of any kind occurs in your life. But grief is not the end. In fact, the process of grief is what leads you to a new beginning. Sometimes, the beginning that you have been pleading, praying, and crying for.

Your storms, setbacks, struggles, and bad situations come at certain points in your life to challenge you. First, to see if you are capable of going the distance. Second, to show you what you are made of. Third, to evaluate your skills at coming up with solutions, making sound decisions, and staying the course. When you face your loss, see it for what it really is, and find a solution to bring it to a close, then you are ready. You have to lose in order to gain. Sometimes that gain is for you. Sometimes that gain is to help others who are struggling to comprehend what you already know.

Find Something Familiar to Hold on To

God found me when I was going through my vulnerable times. Every time I have experienced a loss of one kind or another, I have tried to stay in the Word of God. It is the only way I have survived to be quite honest with you. Don't get me wrong. Many times, I was reluctant to do so and even had to force myself to pick up my Bible, much less open it. Nevertheless, it was in the Word of God that I found answers to so many questions.

Mom was gone. I was a mess, again. I got on my knees and cried out to God. I needed to find solace and peace.

The time I spent praying, even if only for a moment, allowed me to find comfort so I could rest. You may not feel like praying or seeking God when you are grieving from loss, but that is the time to really push through without stopping. It is in your moments of deep pain that you should be even more eager and passionate for all things that pertain to God. I can say that now, but when you are grieving, the first thing that goes is your passion for anything.

When you feel that everything is gone you have to find something familiar to hold on to. For me, God was my familiar. I knew that God's presence always follows His word, so I held on tight. When you know you are not alone, you have hope. That familiar person or thing will let you have peace in the midst of your storm. It was God's promises that preserved my sanity.

Find Someone to Talk To

The first year and a half after mom died, I walked around in a fog. Each day I went through the motions, got up, exercised, showered, ate, went to work, did my work, made conversation with my co-workers, chatted, and smiled when needed. I was sad, but I pushed my sadness back so I could function. My co-workers knew to give me a wide berth. They knew I was grieving the loss of my mother. They knew that it was better to do business as usual rather than say something that would trigger my tears. They could not handle that. Then I came home, and I slept.

Your mind will play games with you. Sometimes there will be guilt. You torment yourself, wondering if you did enough. You will get confused, asking yourself if you could have done something else or different. I went through so many dark days and even darker nights with my brain working overtime trying to make sense of it all. It was at night that the voices got louder, and I would toss and turn. Always restless. Just hovering on the brink of sleep.

When you are living in a dark environment you are going to need help in order to see your way out. You have to trust someone to help you get through the fog, cloud, and darkness that has enveloped you. It could be a therapist, a close friend, a group of like-minded individuals, or, in my case, it was God. In your dark, fog-filled, sad state, you have to talk to someone. You have to listen to others talk. You need to hear the gentle reminders, even though many times you feel alone and deserted. You need to hear that soft voice whispering, through your tears, *"I AM WITH YOU."*

I Forgive You – I Forgive Me

Grieving is painful. The pain is unexpected and deeply felt by you alone. It is not physical pain that you can touch or see. No, this pain causes mental suffering because someone or something so precious to you has gone and cannot be replaced. Yes, you are mourning, but it goes deeper than that, you are grief stricken. We all experience pain. It is inevitable. Human pain, the sort that lingers, is always present either in your face, or in the background. It never leaves you. Just writing the words in this book have brought up strong memories, painful emotions, and feelings I thought had been subside. Not so. Not yet. There was one more step to take.

To be free from pain there has to be forgiveness. Along with reconciling the unfinished business, I had to forgive. And not just forgive, but I also had to let go. I had to let go of all the disappointments, losses, letdowns, and distrust. I had to forgive everyone who had hurt me or caused me pain. I had to do this so that I could heal. You have to understand, grieving is about healing. It is also about loving, again. There will be scars and painful memories that will always want to come and remind you of your past and even try to make you feel guilty, but they too will subside.

When you forgive, you are paving the way for you to live your life complete. Your body and spirit can heal from the void that has been left from your loss, but you have to want it badly and you have to act. That action includes forgiveness. You want to be set free from the pain of the past. The person is dead and buried, it is time to let go. Your spouse has moved out and moved on. The company has folded and no longer exists. The hateful words that were spoken are now a distant memory. Forgive him, her, or them. Forgive so that you can be free of the struggles and pain of the past. And when you forgive you open the door for peace to come in.

You Must Live

Any kind of loss is overwhelming. I've experienced loss before and got back up. In fact, each time I experienced loss I grieved. When mom died, this was the big one. This was what I feared the most and because of that, the impact was great. I wanted to withdraw from the world. For 4 years and 9 months I was going through the motions of life, but I was not living. And who was I hurting the most by locking myself up in a cave and hiding?

The fear of living again almost always follows the big one. Days, weeks, and months go by and you cannot find the will or desire to get back to the act of living. Yet, live you must. You have to hold on to something that is familiar, so you don't lose yourself. You have to find someone you can trust to talk to, so you don't feel alone and isolated. More importantly, you have to learn to forgive so you can heal.

You may be wondering why you are going through your ordeal. I can tell you that you are here for a purpose. When your moment arrives, you will know. Your eyes will be open so you can see clearly. You will know what you must do. It is by no means easy, but you can be happy again. You can have dreams. You can set goals, and you will feel again.

Loss. You cannot just get over it. Sometimes you have to wait. And sometimes you need a moment alone to grieve.

OVERCOMER

About Pangeline Edwards

Pangeline Edwards is an author and speaker in the field of self-development. Over the past 20 years she has focused on helping people deal with unexpected change in their life through her message "Kick Fear Now". She often reminds her audience that most people will experience immense change at various points in their lives. These changes are often followed by doubt and fear.

Ms. Edwards teaches from experience. She knows what it is like to live a life filled with fear. It took her a while but, little by little, she found out that fear loses its weakness when you bring it out in the open. *Kick Fear to the Curb: 5 Action Steps for a Courageous You* was her first book on the issue of unrealistic fear and a culmination of her extensive work on the subject.

Ms. Edwards mission is to EDUCATE! ENGAGE! EMPOWER! She believes that if the next phase of your life is going to be purposeful then you must stop doing the same thing over and again. She wants you to embrace your true value by overcoming and living the victorious life.

Ms. Edwards holds a Master of Theology from Lighthouse Christian College and Master of Emergency Management from the University of Richmond. She is a cum laude graduate of City University of New York – Brooklyn College; holds double Bachelors in Religion and Business, Management & Finance. She is a certified pastoral member of the Sarasota Academy of Christian Counselors.

Website: www.kickfearnow.com

CHAPTER 8

The Big M

By Mayra Nieves

One morning I woke up to the beautiful surprise that it was snowing. I had been in the snow before, but I had never seen snowflakes fall. I got up and went outside the apartment where I was staying to touch them and to pick them up in my hands. Everything was cover in snow. It was 19 degrees outside, but I did not mind the cold, instead it felt exciting. I had never been to Washington State before and it became an unforgettable experience. Although I missed my husband and my kids, in that moment everything was perfect. I felt an inner peace that I had not felt in a long time.

Do you wonder how did I got to Washington?

It resulted from a situation of despair and the need for hope. You see, a few years before making this decision, I was going through the **Big M**, "MENOPAUSE".

WOW, I wrote it, "Menopause." So many people prefer not to speak about it and many women prefer to go through it alone. That was not an option for me, I had to seek the help of doctors, but the truth is that I never got the help I was looking for. I was damaging the relationships with all those I loved.

Now I look back and I am in awe of how I had the strength to get out of such a dark season in my life. What I am certain about, even to this day is that I had the mental resolve to know at that the time that I had to get out of the situation.

Let me take you back a bit when it all started. I was 43, and I would later learn that I already had, what is referred to as, "Premature Menopause." The doctor that finally diagnosed it told me the symptoms of the "Menopause" could last up to 10 years.

Ten years, no, it cannot be, not me!

Menopause what is that?

The doctor(s) explained that it was cause by a hormonal deficiency that happens when a woman's body starts losing its estrogen. As a result, the woman begins to experience internal and external changes that are outside her control. Some of the possible symptoms are Fatigue, Weight Gain, Hot Flashes, Insomnia, Depression, Skin Changes, Low Sex Drive, Muscle Loss, Irritability, Memory Loss, Hair Loss, Vaginal Dryness, Weak Bones, Mood Changes, Night Sweats, Anxiety, Brain Fog, just to mention some.

Now what...

In my case, I started with Hot Flashes in the middle of the night. Many nights I couldn't sleep, and I was up until 3:00 a.m. or 5:00 a.m. I went to see an OBGYN doctor and he told me I was too young to be started on some medication and besides, they didn't believe I was having these symptoms.

OVERCOMER

When the symptoms got worse, I started taking over the counter Estrogen but after a few months, they will no longer worked. I returned to the doctors several times over the next two years, until finally they tested me, and it turned out that I was already in the middle of menopause and that I had been for some time.

Knowing somehow made me feel better, and it led me to believe that, now I was going to get the help, the help I was looking for all this time. I even thought I'd be out of all of this soon; how wrong I was. The symptoms were getting stronger every day and nothing I tried turned out better than what I was already taking.

In addition to the first effects of the Big M, I was barely sleeping, even though I was taking sleeping medication. I started to have a constant ringing in my ear mostly at night cause by the imbalance of my hormones. I guess I would collapse from pure exhaustion. This affected me at work because I could not wake up early in the mornings to work or take care of the family. In addition, the depression too was getting worse every day. There were many times I locked myself in my room without going out for several hours and crying because I was not feeling well. I lost so many hours and days of being with my children who were now teenagers, (Giovanni, Omayra and Michael) and all the while, I still did not understand what was happening to me.

I was not able to explain what I didn't understand myself.

I isolated from my friends, because I did not want anyone to know what was wrong with me. However, despite my behavior, they were always there for me even though they didn't quite understand what was wrong with me. Through all these years, they have been there at all times to support me.

The hormonal imbalance was so difficult to manage that I could not even leave the house, I felt tired and sleepy most of the day. My body did not respond to anything, the pills were doing me more harm than good and none of the doctors gave me a solution. They just changed the pill to creams, to lotions, injections, or tablets.

For those who have never heard this term "MENOPAUSA", it is not only for mature women. More and more young women are diagnosed with this disease for many different reasons. If only it were for the Hot Flashes and nothing more it would not have been so difficult, but aside from those effects there were other physical and psychological effects as well.

Who would say, I have always been a cheerful and adventurous person with a passion for life! In those past moments I felt like the world was ending and all I just wanted was feel good again.

I realized that I could no longer work with clients; my attitude was not the right one. By then the Real Estate business was at its worst as the market fell. Customers were aggressive, they did not want to talk to the realtors and the banks did not want to do much for them.

A disaster!

Many realtors retired from the profession, but I did not want to leave what it took me so long to build.

OVERCOMER

My relationship with my husband was deteriorating, daily getting worse. Our communication was truly little; he also had his work concerns because I was almost unemployed.

The storm arrived; well actually, it was more of a tornado!

The market dropped out and we all lost our jobs and savings.

Few years passed, and I felt better, but then without notice it started again, all the same symptoms. I could not talk to anyone because they also were dealing with the effects of the years that followed the American financial disaster. All my friends had financial and family situations.

Time went by and before I knew it, I found myself in conversations with women, who now were going through something similar. They shared with me something I had never been told by any doctor yet, "REPLACEMENT HORMONE THERAPY". I had always been afraid to put anything in my body that was not natural. When I mentioned it to the doctors, they did not recommend this possible solution, but they also did not give me a better option.

Before going through the big M… I had never had any diseases. I was an extremely healthy person and the only thing I was taking were vitamins.

Time passed and the kids were already in college, now it was just my husband and I alone in a big house. He has always been my best friend and partner in life. He understood a little bit about what was happening to me, but we could not find the right help. One day, I told him, "I want to get out of the real estate business, and I want to go away for a while to study another career." He never hesitated to help me, and the decision was made. I decided to go back to school and go to Flight Attendant training for few months. It was the career I always wanted to pursue as a young woman but because of the children never had the opportunity. We thought this was the best chance to take a break from both of us. Would give us the time to work on our marriage and to allow me to focus on myself again. We found a Flight Attendant school in Washington State and I applied for school. They accept me and I left for almost two months.

I know it might sound crazy, but it was the best decision of my life. That decision saved my marriage and my life.

I was there from late October to early December. I was able to study and pass my exams with 100%. I discovered that the stress of my past work was hurting me, so I took time to get to know myself again. I shared the apartment with other roommates, and we became very good companions.

It was late autumn and the beginning of winter and the city would look beautiful. It was so relaxing to see the leaves falling and I felt the peace I needed at that time. The trees were completely yellow and a few weeks later they were covered by snow.

I started studying, going to the gym every day, and reading or walking in the afternoons. Sometimes we would go out for dinner and then to study at night. Many times, I did FaceTime with my husband and the kids. We even celebrated that year's Thanksgiving through

FaceTime. I still remember and will never forget how my husband put the iPad at the end of the table, so I was part of the dinner celebration. It was the first time in my life that I was not there for them, but they understood it was necessary.

God only knows that thanks to him and his grace and the love and patience of my husband I am here and in good health. I love you!

When I returned to Florida, I felt clearer and was in a better state emotionally. It was time for me to see a specialist again. This time I knew I had to do whatever was needed for my sake. I went to the OBGYN specialist on Bio-identical Hormone Replacement treatment, now I know had to do it for me.

We decided to sell the house and move to something smaller near the beach and start fresh again. It was not easy, but we managed to work on our marriage, and I went back to real estate.

Through state-of-the-art diagnostic hormone testing, using blood and urine testing, they were able to determine my hormone levels and my unique bioidentical hormone needs.

Every three months I had to get my treatment, "pellets" implant to keep hormones at the right levels. I had to do the implant replacement every 3 months and not go over 1 day otherwise my body would start to manifest deterioration for the next few days. I did not care how much it cost, (by the way it was not and is not covered by medical plans) or how much it hurt but it had to be done. My body had a total imbalance and gradually I was feeling normal again.

The new normal!

Among the side effects of the treatment was the possibility of cancer among many other effects... but I never thought that I'd be one within that small percent.

It was already two years into the Bio-identical Hormonal replacement treatment, and I was feeling super good and strong. It was time to do my follow up, Mammogram, as I did in the past, but this time I took a little longer to go. I made the appointment before we left for Spain for our Christmas vacation. When we returned from the holidays, I received a call from the hospital to go in and repeat some of the breast exams again. I did not think anything of it because I was feeling great. After many mammograms, sonograms, blood test, and other studies on February 14, 2017 my doctor called me to tell me that I had Breast Cancer.

I did not only have the Big M, but now the Big C. How lucky was I.

I remember it like it was today, and my only worry was for my family. I love them very much, and they had walked through my battle with the Big M; and now this.

From then on, I spent few months doing test and more test. I had a Lumpectomy done but thanks to GOD I did not have to go through Chemotherapy and at the end was only required to complete 30-days of Radiation treatment.

Some doctors have said that it may had been caused by the Bio-identical hormone replacement and the way my body processes it. Others said the cancer could have been caused by what was going on in my life during those years. True or not, if it were not for the Bio-identical hormone treatment, I don't know what would have happened to me.

After going through those years of madness due to "menopause", there was nothing that could be worse.

I fought the cancer and won! Few months after my dad passed away...but that is a different story.

Today, I know I can fight against whatever comes in life.

I am not a superwoman, but I have to fight for my health like. I am still dealing with few symptoms but most of them are gone.

Here is what I have to do to take back control of my mind and my body.

1. Keep my mind positive at all times.

2. Surround myself with positive people.

3. Advocate helping women that are going through menopause.

4. Be open minded to accept new changes and challenges

5. Enjoy and practice reading, yoga, meditation, exercise, walks on the beach.

6. Love the ones around me and show gratitude at all times and believe in something   bigger.

I learned to be patience and have compassion for others. I love my husband and enjoy spending time with him, my kids, and my grandkids. I learned to accept my past and moved on to my better present.

As a cancer patient, I have to take a pill for the next few years. I still have some of those menopause effects mostly the hot flashes, so I use less clothes or open the fridge more often.   I cannot take any more hormones for the rest of my life. However, life keeps going and I have to get up every day and feel the grace of the VICTORY AND NOT BE THE VICTIM OF MY PAST.

"Physiological data and clinical outcomes demonstrate that bioidentical hormones are associated with lower risks, including the risk of breast cancer and cardiovascular disease, and are more efficacious than their synthetic and animal-derived counterparts," states the report. Copyright © 2019 Body Logic MD

My message today to all women is that, "Do not hesitate to look for help when you know something is wrong."

As one of the doctors told me: "You all are going through hormones changes from the time you had your first period. Then go through anticonception pills and pregnancies and you expect to feel the same".

OVERCOMER

If you want to ready more about this topic, https://www.onhealth.com/content/1/hormone_imbalance_si gns_symptoms

https://u.bodylogicmd.com/bioidentical-hormone-replacement-therapy/

About Mayra Nieves

Born and raised in Puerto Rico, Mayra Nieves is still very much in touch with her roots. She moved from P.R. right after getting married to her sweetheart and moved to a Navy Base in Italy were, they spent few years. After her husband retired from the USA NAVY, they transferred to South Florida where they have been for over 20 years.

President and Founder of the Fort Lauderdale Hispanic Alliance group. Her goal is to inspire professional Latinos to work together, promote their business and get involved in the community they live and work in to create a better tomorrow.

Mayra has a Bachelor's Degree in Business Administration. She started in the business of Financing and Real Estate right after moving to Florida. Currently, she is a successful Real Estate agent with the Remax Consultants Realty group in Fort Lauderdale, Florida. Love to help and get involved with Non-profit groups.

Her biggest accomplishment is the relationship with her husband of 35 years and with her three kids and grandkids.

Mayra has completed a few leadership programs including Tony Robbins, Landmark Forum and others.

Mayra's Vision: Create awareness within the women's community to be stronger as we get older.

OVERCOMER

Email: Mayra.Nieves@remax.net

Website: www.MayraSellsHomes.com

CHAPTER 9

"Learning to Live Loved"

By Debbie Csutoros

Have you ever felt like you were living two different lives in one body?

Have you ever given away your power to the negative words or behaviors of others, worse yet believed them?

For most of my young life, I grew up believing I was unloved, but if you had asked me, I would have told you differently. There was a lot of dysfunction on the surface of my life that I buried. I believed I was full of joy and the life of the party. I denied the pain of my parents' traumatic divorce, generations of alcoholism and secrets of abuse. If any of this resonates with you, then by the time you finish this story you will see what I never did, until now. How I learned to battle the disparity between how others treated me, how I treated myself and the life I hunger for. Many experiences exposed the unloved places in my heart I could not reach. But learning that in fact I am loved, is allowing me to share with you a few of these experiences and how I battle each day to live-loved.

Question

Do you believe, "There has to be more to life than this?" (Reflect and write your answer)

_____

_____

_____

_____

_____

_____

I am not sure if this was a sigh or an audible question. Maybe it was just a thought as I sat in the bathroom after a long night partying my freshman year of college. What I do know is the brokenness I felt. This question was a cry from a deeper place inside my soul I had not acknowledged. Was it sadness, pain, guilt or just pure shame? I was grasping for something I wasn't sure existed. Was there something more to this life or was this it? This couldn't be all there was. Nothing I did seemed to satisfy me. I felt so exhausted and rejected. I was beginning to lose the youthful covering of joy that seemed to sustain me up to this point. I finished up in the bathroom and began unconsciously looking for something to fill the void. This time I did something different. I went into my suitemate's room and pulled a book off her shelve. I thumbed through it quickly. "Nope this isn't it." I returned it to the shelf and went off to class. When I returned there it was, that exact book I had earlier skimmed through was sitting on my bed! Weird. I picked it up again and did not put it down for months. I devoured it, "The Power of Positive Thinking" by Norman Vincent Peale. I read it. I wrote about it. I repeated the hope it contained for me as if it were my new drug. This began a habit of writing and documenting my life experiences.

The Answer

The book often referenced Bible verses. I had never read the Bible before and I didn't own one. But this book that had reappeared on my bed that day encouraged the repeating of one sentence. "I can do all things through Jesus Christ who strengthens me". (If you have heard Jesus stories before and want to tune this out, I get that. Just keep reading, there is something here for you). Returning home that summer, I ran into some old friends. While catching up on high school days, they mentioned that our friend Michael was now a "Jesus freak." I laughed with them and said, "No way, not Mike." But inside something stirred. I thought, "Jesus, who is this Jesus?" I have to talk to Michael and find out more." We ended up spending the summer together and through amazing experiences I learned about this Jesus. Michael would tell me he came to earth in miraculous ways to rescue me. He loved me and died in my place so I could be forgiven. His perfect life and blood could reconnect me to the God of love. I didn't understand it all but somewhere inside me I knew I needed rescuing. I hated myself. I hated the things I had done and the things others had done to me. I wanted to be forgiven and empowered to change and I asked this Jesus to help me. Most of all I wanted love. A seed was planted somewhere deep inside me that summer. I began staying home and I started drawing pictures I would find of Jesus, lots of them. The drawing lasted about a year, but as life's responsibilities increased, the drawings were put away. Some joy had returned, but unbeknownst to me, the toxic roots of unprocessed grief and pain remained.

Love Speaks

Fifteen years later I was sitting on the passenger side of my SUV with a blank sketchpad in my lap. My well-worn art box was within arms' reach on the backseat. I was angry with God that day. He had led me back to the memory of drawing and said: "That's what I want you to do." "What, draw?" That made no sense to me. I wrestled with all this for quite a few weeks, but I knew it was time for a change, so I followed a voice I was learning to hear. Sitting in my truck that day I asked, "Well? What now?" I know it may sound crazy, but I heard a whisper: "Draw yourself." "What? I can't draw myself." This instruction made me doubtful and angry. I didn't understand. But I heard it again, a gentle but firm insistence, "Draw yourself."

"Okay, I'll draw myself," I snapped. I was thinking, "*This is a waste of time.*" I sketched a pretty one-dimensional portrait of myself as I looked through the re-view mirror. Still angry, I lifted the pad heavenward and cried out, "Look at this, this is no masterpiece. What are you doing?" The words I heard next were: "No, *you* are my masterpiece." Immediately I broke into tears. I had never heard anything so impactful. God was speaking to me and I knew it without a doubt. These four words touched me so deeply. I realized in that moment I believed nothing close to this about myself. Forgiven or not, inside I was still that girl in college, the young child of my youth believing a lie that I was flawed. I had read and studied the Bible for years by now, but I had not dealt with the roots of my past and that pain that was beginning to surface in that moment. There was a disconnection between God's voice and the beliefs that had shaped me. I was recognizing I didn't know who I was from God's perspective. The pain I was feeling was wrapped in love. I was beginning to grieve because God knew I needed to. I could not have taken myself to this place. It says in the Bible he sets captives free and he was initiating freedom for me in those moments. Learning to hear him like this became my passion and I knew the Bible had something to do with it. So every day I fought to not quit, to hear him again and follow with all I had.

The Battle

I began working over the next 10 years as an artist. Who knew? God was revealing me to myself; I am his masterpiece and an artist. My friend Marge inspired the first picture I drew as I began again. I still didn't know what I was doing but she encouraged me to sit down and ask God to draw something through me. I remember sitting on my couch and drawing a simple pine tree I could see in my neighbor's yard. I titled it "The Struggle to Abide". This has become my mantra; the *"Struggle to Abide, the Battle to Bloom."* This is the battle to live loved and not quit on myself. It's battling to do the hard work of believing, often without being able to see or feel it's true. Battling to remain in God's presence daily to hear his voice is how I am learning to live loved today. I created many beautiful pieces of artwork in those days. My company was called Desiring Hearts, Inc. I continued to battle with how I saw myself. I created hand mirrors to remind those who bought them that they are created in God's image. They were called "Reflections of His Glory". Now I see those 10 years as God's divine plan to ingrain this fact into my broken heart. The lenses through which I viewed my body and myself were skewed. I thought if I just kept myself looking thin and put together on the outside, all would be well. Without continuing the battle to abide and be still with Him my shackles would have remained. I was learning I have to let God and the Bible examine my beliefs, thoughts, and heart for change.

Hidden in me were so many painful life experiences. It was so much easier to examine my waistline than my subconscious beliefs. Eventually the lie was exposed; skinny equaled loved! That was huge for me. This was a core issue in my life and God was rooting it out. We were digging our pool in the backyard around this time. We had two trees that needed to be removed. The root balls were massive. They had to dig them out with a bulldozer. Before they hauled them off, I walked out into the backyard to get a closer look. As I was examining them, I heard God say; "That's what I am taking out of your life." I wept again.

Comrades

While pressing into the artwork I remained connected to the Bible through different groups and studies. Eventually, I began meeting with just two friends each week. We grew to be confidants. Our trust and love for each other grew as we shared our deepest struggles and joys weekly. We made commitments to each other that we would read the Bible a little each day and document our time with God writing in journals. After a few years meeting at a local coffee shop we realized we were hearing God. He was speaking into the hidden places of their hearts, like He was mine. We were witnesses to this in each other's lives. We could see God at work and hear him with increased clarity as we got more and more vulnerable with each other. We realized having a safe place to verbally process life with scripture was a gift. The only question we ask ourselves every day was **"What did God say to you today?"** We have been meeting weekly now for over 17 years still asking the same question every day.

Peace

God never failed to provide peace when I was really struggling. I was with my family on vacation. I woke up wrestling with something and I needed to spend some time with God. So, I sent the family off ahead of me and I would catch up with them later. I was reading in John chapter 20:26. Jesus had just been crucified and his disciples were afraid they would be next, so they locked themselves in a room. They didn't understand why He had to die. They had left everything to follow him. As they were discussing their next move, it says, "Though the doors were locked Jesus came and stood among them and said, "Peace be with you."" I stopped reading at that point and thought, *"He walked through locked doors? This is supernatural!"* As I began to write in my journal, I was writing about how Jesus had risen from the dead and now he could walk through these doors. Then God whispered to me, *"Debbie I am able to walk through the locked doors of your heart. I am going to places inside your heart that you can't get to, places you don't even know are there."* Then he said to the disciples; "Peace be with you" He brought me that same peace. I looked up the definition of peace that day. It means among other things; freedom of the mind…in Hebrew it means; shalom, translated, "enough"! He was my enough that day. He is enough.

The Process

Hearing God has revealed a process, which has led us to create a ministry called YadaFactor. "Yada" is Hebrew and means; to know. God knows us and makes himself available for us to know him. Factor is a mathematical term to express the exponential factor of knowing God through hearing. It's a sacred rhythm that allows God to enter our soul. I invite you into this process. Please take a look at the website. **YadaFactor.com** There is a free eBook you can download to get started as our gift. Begin asking God your questions. If you're like me and don't know this Jesus, ask him. Start reading just enough to digest, then stop and begin writing to him, talk to him. Document your days with the date. Ask him everything, anything and keep reading and writing no matter what.

When we write we use a method called **S.O.A.P,** which is an acronym for **S**cripture, **O**bservation, **A**pplication, **P**rayer. You will need a journal and a Bible to get started. I have found he is always waiting to love me. Don't underestimate even five minutes of stillness with God. When you miss a day, week or even a month, go back. His love trumps your performance that's what humbles me the most. He always loves me! Actually, it's how I've learned real love. Real love is unconditional and sacrificial.

The Choice

God heard the cry of my heart in that college bathroom. Trauma, pain and grief would have remained hidden for a lifetime if it wasn't for God's love and promise to heal the broken-hearted. I will battle to live from His truth of loved every day. Living loved is a daily journey of discovery for me. Like when I see my anger in disproportion to my situation, I know something else is bothering me. When I begin to put too much attention on my body, I know there is more going on than what meets the eye. I have learned to face my faults and failures by asking God and others to forgive me. I am no longer a victim to the behaviors or neglect of others, most of the time. I have found my worth and value as a beloved daughter of my Father in heaven. I have learned how important it is to keep practicing vulnerability with God, others and myself. It will never come naturally. I have found the 'Why' for my life and work. ***If God can enable me to live loved he can do that for anyone. You are my why, that you might live loved today.*** We will no longer be held captive by "unloved," shut up beliefs that want to destroy and steal our lives. Each day we get to choose how to live and today I choose to live loved.

You can check out **livelovedtoday.com**

About Debbie Csutoros

Debbie's life call is "creating connection". Her passion is to help people hear God's voice with increased clarity. She is passionate for the Bible and learning to live a life that reflects the astonishing glory of her heavenly Father. Debbie is Executive Director and Co-founder of YadaFactor. She is also an artist, writer, speaker and a licensed Realtor.

She is a mother of two grown daughters, Rachel and Nicole, and wife to the love of her life, Steven William.

CHAPTER 10

FIRST LOVE YOURSELF (F.L.Y.)

By: Grace Holden

More than 3,000 adolescent girls were studied, the result from the research revealed that seven out of 10 believe that they're not good enough. They felt they weren't beautiful enough, bright enough, slim enough or even deserve to be loved. This study also revealed that 75 percent of girls with low self-esteem engaged in "Negative activities such as disordered eating, cutting, bullying, smoking, or drinking when feeling bad about themselves."[1] What else could be expected from living in constant unhappiness with oneself?

The starting point of true happiness and fulfillment in life is to first love yourself. Which is exactly how each of us were born, until…one day outside factors came along and shattered our self-esteem and our self-worth. Self-esteem in not a vacuum it can be snatched from you, slowly and/or instantly.

Ask yourself this:

Do you value yourself?

Or

Do you devalue who you are and don't know why or how?

One of the biggest mistakes you'll ever make is to dissolve subtly into low self-worth. Devaluing yourself is the product of focusing on what you are not, forgetting what you are-- your uniqueness and identity.

You Are Worth More!

You see, one of the golden rules to first loving yourself is to have a correct and truthful definition of your worth and to actually like yourself. Most likely, you cannot price something correctly unless you first discover it's actual worth.

So, have you discovered your worth?

What do you attach your importance to?

Is it something temporal or a clear description of your real value?

Understand that your worth is not, and should not be defined by your education, the man or woman in your life, your high paying job, your breath-taking beauty, your company of friends, your lucrative highly demanded business, your fat bank account, your blissful marriage, social status or even your past, good or bad. A lot of times, these factors change. For instance, you may lose your job, the business may collapse, and your spouse may leave.

But, if you attach your worth and relevance in life to some of these fleeting factors, then you may become trapped in an endless cycle of dissatisfaction. The popular American actor and playwright, Harvey Forbes Fierstein, once said, *"Never be bullied into silence. Never allow yourself to be made a victim. Accept no one's definition of your life, but define yourself."*

LIKE A LILY AMONG THORNS

I had to find myself and fall in love with my self—I was left alone with myself often; and I realized I was the only one that never left my side. I had neglected my responsibility of showering myself with love, attention, and affection at the very moment I needed it the most; when I experienced the hurt, disappointment, separation and singleness.

One day I resolved—never again will I do that to myself, dependent on external validation of who I am and what my worth is. I will fall in love again, but this time with myself. Because, the days of seeking acceptance and approval when I could have satisfied my soul's yearning are over. This marked my moment of illumination, when is yours?

FIRST LIKE YOURSELF (FLY)

The first step to loving yourself is *liking* yourself. According to Merriam Webster, the word *like* means to enjoy, get pleasure from, to regard with favor or to feel affection for something or someone. It also means to enjoy being with someone. This entails becoming your own best friend, appreciating your opinion, establishing your value system, discovering all the dynamics of your character, and being content to spend time alone with yourself. It means preferring your company above all else and having a good relationship with yourself.

If your happiness depends on the people around you, please expect that your emotions will drive and may cause instability of confidence. Mood swings can be triggered easily, don't be surprised. You might eventually fall victim of self-sabotage and not liking you.

But if you can be happy and be satisfied with yourself, when people leave, your emotions will not be left shattered. Also, if your happiness is dependent upon your job, business or some material thing, when they are no more, what are you going to do about it? But one constant thing is that when your genuine happiness comes from you, you definitely don't have anything to lose. Of as Oprah Winfrey has said, "You don't have anything to give that you don't have." The starting point of receiving the love of others is to begin by loving yourself. Self-love is the best thing you can gift yourself if you want to know what true happiness means.

I can only love you to the same degree that I love me.

To love you, I have to begin with liking and respecting myself first. I am the main character in the script, and I can only, "Love my neighbor as myself." In other words, I am to love my neighbor just as I do myself.

Have you taken time to know yourself?

What makes you happy or sad?

Do you find humor and excitement when you're alone?

Do you talk to yourself when your mood is down and set yourself straight when you overstep boundaries?

Can you say you have a relationship with yourself?

Again, do you even like yourself?

Most people have not cultivated a friendship with themself. They don't think they are excellent company and they do not even like the sound of their own voice. They believe they are dull and boring; because of this, they continually seek other people whom they think are exciting and full of life. This self-dislike is never helpful.

In redeveloping self-love, you need to come to a place where you respect and admire what you've been through, who you are right now, and the person you are becoming. When you do this, you'll have healthy self-esteem that will develop into resolute self-worth.

FALL IN LOVE WITH *ME* AGAIN

You were born with everything you need inside of you. Developing self-love starts with knowing yourself; you cannot accept what you do not know. There are several ways to get to know yourself.

1. You can start by taking the time to listen to yourself without judging or criticizing.

2. Take a walk on a cool evening or take time to visit beautiful places all by yourself.

3. You can date yourself. Go out for an on-purpose expensive lunch. Get prepared for it like you would if you were going on a romantic date.

OVERCOMER

On a date with yourself and by yourself, try to fall in love with "me" all over again. Start doing all kinds of stuff you could have done while you were with your friends, and your journey will begin.

A date for one could be as romantic as having a date with someone. Take this quick idea as an example, on a perfect evening, set up the dinner table for yourself, with candles and perfumes and even flowers, make everywhere as romantic as you would make it if you had a date with someone else. You could order any meal of your choice or better still make your own delicacies. You could go further in dressing gorgeously, and the general idea is falling in love with yourself. You could ask yourself questions that will reveal more about who you are. Place yourself in a position of wanting to be your own partner. What a fantastic evening that would be!

But sadly, not everyone believes in loving themselves first. Many are dealing with self-doubt, which may be due to some trauma or pain that they experienced. Some people are hurt to the extent that they now think hurting is normal. So, they naturally pick on others.

We often put ourselves against someone else in terms of competing and comparison. You should understand that you are unique and you can't successfully be someone else. Besides if you are not you, then who would be you? In this type of situation making yourself the best you can be might just be the best solution. Stop comparing yourself to others, don't make their lives be your standard.

Self-dislike or self-doubt could possibly lead to body shaming. And most times it is challenging to view the positive side, especially with mind bullies. Why don't you just ignore what people say, what they see, what they want you to be, and focus on being more presentable and give no room for their talks? Like mentioned earlier, work on making yourself the better version of yourself.

RECAPTURE YOUR SELF WORTH

Dr. Christina Hibbert, a Clinical Psychologist and founder of the Arizona Postpartum Wellness Coalition, states it more clearly, *"Self-esteem is what we think and feel and believe about ourselves. Self-worth is recognizing 'I am greater than all of those things.' It is a deep knowing that I am of value, that I am loveable, necessary to this life, and of incomprehensible worth."* [2]

Another strategy to begin the journey to loving yourself, is to start thinking positively, doing things that makes you feel good, and believing in yourself as a best friend does – all this will boost your self-esteem. Recognize the differences though between self-esteem and self-worth. From my perspective, self-worth translates into unconditional love for who you are.

Yes, at the initial stages, you can settle for going by how you feel, the thoughts you think, and your strong opinions about yourself –all that needs to change in order to boost your low-esteem to rise. However, self-respect and worth are products of increasing self-love, and it will give you the ability to walk out of toxic relationships and situations without compromise. When you know your worth, you won't let anyone treat you anyhow. You don't need to beg for love, you don't need to stoop so low to seek attention, you are a priceless gem, nobody has the right to hold your life for ransom. You are loved, you are cherished, you are lovely, and you are priceless, you are essential, these are the words that should resonate in your mind.

FLY LIKE A BUTTERFLY

Now, do you know why you should grow your self-love? How does it feel to live in a chameleon's skin? How does it feel to always reflect the desires of others while you drown your happiness?

You must have seen an excited butterfly, freely flying and flopping her beautiful self. Chameleons can be colorful, but do they look happy?

Truly, adaptive skills are perfected when you don't love yourself. But you're meant to do more than adapt. You were made to thrive you were made to overcome as your authentic you!

SELF-LOVE WHILE HURTING

More often than not, the issues of self-hate and self-love can be traced back to someone's family's past. For many people, their formative years were rough seasons that negatively affected their self-image. The most impressionable hurts that influence the way people feel about themselves, as a adult was caused by the way their parents saw and treated them, as kids. Maybe you were labeled throughout childhood as dull, annoying, unworthy, ugly, not-good-enough, or even unwanted. All these negative words said over you, can constitute hurts that ingrain self-derogatory images into the mind.

Do you have hurt from your past?

Can you trace it back to your childhood?

Was it something that was said to you?

Or

Evil done to make you feel worthless?

I believe, no matter what has caused hurt to your self-love, it can be healed and restored back to health. You can overcome it.

CAN YOU KEEP A SECRET?

I understand people might have said the meanest things to you, but why store up all that junk in your mind? The thing about not loving yourself is that you can become desperate for any kind of external affection. As a result, you might start telling others the worst about yourself to gain pity and sympathy. This might only bring more hurt instead of the comfort you desire because not everyone is equipped to hear your darkest secrets. And instead of depending on others to love and heal your wounds, you must ask yourself some difficult questions.

Is it possible that you can become hurt so much because you're trying to save someone else?

Can it be that you don't believe you're worthy of being saved?

Earlier I said, self-care first is critical. Stop trying to play the hero who dies for others because you have nothing to live for. Pay attention to your wounds until they heal. Think about it, do you want someone as messed up as you to save you? Of course not!

OVERCOMER

Furthermore, your lack of self-love might be the root of your pain. This is because when you love yourself, others can tell. You determine the way you're treated. Thus, you can devalue yourself without knowing it and open the door for a world of hurt.

REGAINING YOUR SELF-WORTH

What do you think?

Abraham Lincoln once said, *"it is difficult to make a man miserable while he feels worthy of himself."* If this is true, how do your de-clutter your mind and regain self-worth? First, you must be ready to clear up your mental and emotional clutter. Manage your daily stress, let go of the past, and never think you can please everyone!

Now, let's get into running through a quick check-up in regaining your self-worth.

HEART AND MIND CHECK

Stephen Richards stated, *"Reality is a projection of your thoughts or the things you habitually think about."* Running a heart-check is critical to regaining and retaining your self-worth. Here is a Proverb I love **"Guard your heart** *with all diligence, for out of it flows the* **issues of life**.*"* The direction of your life is determined by the content of your heart. You need to understand that whatsoever you permit into your heart will eventually find expression in your life! If you have allowed guilt of your past mistakes to settle in your heart, it begins to spill out and your heart bears it, which means your mind has to bear it. Choose to not allow the past pain, traumas, disappoints to run your mind. Lead with your heart.

SPIRIT AND BODY CHECK

You must understand that your happiness is not only dependent on the satisfaction of your body, but also of your spirit. To find rest and fulfillment in life, there is a need for you to pay attention to both your body and spirit! To be creative and productive in life, you need clarity of mind, soul, and body.

You know what?

You must never let anyone lead you into a world of depression because your body shape seems not to please them. You're beautiful the way you are! Your worth should not be determined by what you wear or any brand in vogue. Is there anything about your body that makes you think less human? Perhaps you have a physical deformity, so what? You are beautiful the way you are. Never believe the lie that you are ugly.

Think about what Jim Rohn said—*"Take care of your body. It's the only place you have to live in."* Never allow yourself to be defined by outside forces (people's opinion, criticism, and praises).

FINALLY DISPEL UNFORGIVENESS

Lack of self-love has been proven to be a dominant trait in people who grew up in abusive, tense, and hostile environments. So, how can you move past yesterday into a new day of love? Make the choice first for yourself. The only safe route is to dispel bitterness and unforgiveness. That's what sets you up for success and victory when you battle self-dislike.

Sincerely, going through life is literally impossible without people who will offend you. Yet, you must learn to let go. You have to choose to be so in love with yourself that you won't let in the hurt and bitterness. They don't deserve your peace, guard it jealously. Nobody deserves to make you sad while they walk around without even noticing it. Don't let anyone postpone your happiness, not even yourself. It will be too challenging to walk free through life with a heavy burden of hurt and unforgiveness in your heart. I have previously written and shared the 7-steps to forgiveness. So, live free, live victoriously.

Whether you have your life all fledged out yet or not, you have to first fall in love with you. Delight in taking care of your mind, body, and spirit. For you, require healthy esteem and a strong sense of worth to emerge as the best version of you.

If you're determined to overcome in life, to live a life full of happiness, you must love yourself. As Robert Holden rightly said, "*Happiness is not in things. It's in you!*" Indeed, it is better to know and practice self-love than to lose a limb in search of happiness from people and things. Don't compromise. Don't hold back when you love yourself. You are unconditionally loved, born with love, not contingent on what you did do and not taken away based on what you didn't do. Root yourself to your core, your center and allow this place to always help you find your way back to yourself.

"Let love be the last word and just spread your wings and fly!" -Grace Holden

<u>Citations</u>

[1] https://www.psychalive.org/stop-hating-yourself/

[2] https://positivepsychology.com/self-worth/

About Grace Holden

Author Grace L. Holden is a mother of 5, a lover of people. She was the Victim of multiple traumas before the age of 20! She is a Voice of HOPE sharing her incredible story delivered in the most unique, brilliant and transparent way.

Grace is a multi-passionate Keynote Motivational Speaker, Leadership Expert, and Personal & Executive Coach whose unwavering sense of dedication and no-nonsense approach have earned her the reputation as a down-to- earth strategist in the business space. Throughout the span of over two decades, she has garnered extensive expertise helping people thrive both professionally and personally.

Grace is an unstoppable visionary and a positive force. During her undergraduate years at SPU in Seattle, Grace was severely abused, stabbed and oppressed...and those weren't even her worst traumas. Through all of the seemingly life ending repeated devastations, Grace refused to quit and somehow managed to complete her undergraduate degree in Communications while being a single mother.

Currently, Grace proudly serves as the Founder and CEO of a National and Global Speaking Agency - Real Champions League, LLC. Her Speakers Bureau amplifies voices all over the world including those impacted by trauma in their life. She sits on the Board of The

Elite Foundation as Co-Chair. Her literary work: Dirty, Invincible, Overcomers.

In addition to a Master's Degree in Human Services, she holds a Certified John Maxwell Coach, Trainer, Speaker, and Leader designation. Ultimately, Grace is on a lifelong mission to empower people to find their unique voice, discover their passion, and unlock their hidden potential.

Grace has a heart big enough to fit the world in it and she has the tenacity to be the Catalyst of a Nationwide Movement called Dads Against Dirty.

Grace is destined to unify men and women, boys and girls, survivors, overcomers, concerned organizations and other authors to help bring awareness to the trauma many hide. Join Grace in her dedication and commit to the cause.

Email: info@RealChampionsLeague.com

Website: **GraceLHolden.com and RealChampionsLeague.com**

PART III

The Transition to Change

CHAPTER 11

I Don't Want the Neighbors to Know

But What Did He Do ~~To~~ For You?

By Charmène Vega

It was 8:00 AM on Wednesday, March 27, 2013, in Palmdale, California. The sky was clear, 70 degrees and the sun shined so brightly that it was blinding yet, I felt cold as though a cloud hung over me. I felt a heaviness in my heart, it was hard to breathe, my fingers were cold, and my palms were sweating. As I put one foot in front of the other walking up the stairs, my knees began to buckle. I quickly regained my composure and balance. My best friend, Lynda, turned to me and said, "It's clear *what he did to you*, they will see it." I looked at her raising one eyebrow, clinching my lips together and nodding my head while at the same time saying, "But *what didn't he do*, there is still so much more I don't know and he is quite adept at distorting the truth." Lynda grabbed my hand, began to hug me and whispered in my ear. "Now, is the time to remember what your dad taught you and what you taught your daughters and students, but most of all what you have lived by all these years. *"No, means not that way!"* Regardless of what happens today, you will persevere, and the truth will be told, listened to, heard and you will show others how to overcome adversities gracefully while remaining true to who you are." With that, we walked into the Superior Courthouse County of Los Angeles.

119

OVERCOMER

Once inside the courthouse, we went up to the second floor and sat on the bench outside courtroom A13. While we talked to each other I heard that familiar unnerving sound of deliberate footsteps. It was PMJ (Palter Mendacious Jilter). Anyone who knows him is aware he wears taps on his shoes to announce his approaching. I never looked up as he passed by in front of the two of us. At 8:30 AM, the bailiff began calling out names and allowed us to enter the courtroom where we took our seats waiting for the judge to enter and the bailiff to call the court to order. We sat there for quite a while before the judge called case MQ009463, Vega vs Jilter. I walked forward to the Plaintiff's table and Palter took his position at the Defendants table. After being sworn in, the judge asked me to explain the need for a Permanent Restraining Order.

Reaching down into my oversized purse, pulling out the red folder containing the Temporary Restraining Order, DV-110, additional statements of recent abuse, sworn notarized statements from eyewitnesses, along with pictures; nervously, I described how Palter would come home agitated early in the am after I had gone to sleep, flicking the lights off and on yelling about whatever agitated him, as was his norm. Other times if I started to walk away during his ranting, he would block my way, so I had nowhere to go. While yelling, standing within arm's length of me, pointing his finger at my nose, twirling it within two inches of my face, it made me sweat. He was very aware I did not like anything in my face as at one time I had almost drowned. On numerous occasions he called me, "stupid, an a_ _ hole, naïve", and much worse. He threatened to *hurt me physically* and even said, *you could disappear, and no one would find you, there are plenty of places in the Angeles Crest Forest you know.* To put this in perspective, he is a former football player, 6'3", lifted weights and worked out every day, at the time this was taking place, I was 5'2" and 120 lbs. I'm still 5'2", but... I further explained how I discovered he had manipulated the finances, so my money was always depleted.

Ten years earlier he coaxed me to refinance my home to finance the much-needed repairs with him as the cosigner. He said, "your house belongs to you and your daughters' and I'll sign a Quit Claim. This is just so you qualify for the loan." You guessed it, the Quit Claim never happened, he kept giving excuses which led to heated arguments whenever I asked about it. Eventually, I stopped asking. At one point he said, "I don't want to refinance because I don't want it to *"interfere with what I'm trying to do."* This made no sense. How could me, refinancing my home, interfere with *what he was trying to do?* It became clearer as more situations unfolded, *The WHOLE THING was planned from the very beginning, I, was, <u>targeted</u>. It, was all, a ruse!*

Going back to this first time in court, all he said to the judge was, "Mam, I never touched her." The judge looked at me and SHE said, *"But What Did He Do to You?"* I gave her more examples and once again she said, *"But What Did He Do to You?"* Frustrated, I looked at her in total disbelief, frozen and so stunned that I was speechless. At that moment, if, I said anything, I would have been held in contempt of court, so I just kept quiet and looked at her. The judge then said, "Case Dismissed."

OVERCOMER

While gathering my papers and composure, I glanced at the attorneys sitting in the jury box. Our eyes connected and they mouthed, "sorry." Lynda and I walked quietly out of the courtroom to outside the courthouse and sat on the concrete wall encircling one of the trees. While sitting on the wall, a couple of attorneys, walked over to us shaking their heads and said, "That is a slick suit, wrong venue, don't give up." Lynda asked for their cards which they gave to us. Tears began streaming down my face, once again, Lynda said, "Remember what your dad taught you, No means not that way." I looked at her with tears still running down my face. She looked at me and said, "You know I love you and will always tell you the truth. I just want to say you look like $h!* with your makeup smudged all over your face." We both laughed and I said, "Let me drop you off at home".

What next? Pulling up to the fence at my home, I saw the sign I had posted on the inside of the fence had been ripped down. Palter had previously said to Lynda *"I don't want the neighbors to know."* The message was clear and loud that the sign bothered him and he was not going to stop. However, only a few people knew what was really going on in my life, I kept up my public image. So many women are too ashamed to tell anyone what is going on. Furthermore, there is the denial. It took another close friend and her fiancé (Love Is Foundation) to get me to realize I was being abused. Like so many others I thought you had to be beaten. Given Palter was the former VP of Network Operations for BET (Black Entertainment Television) with all his connections, and ability to collude the truth, I was convinced no one would believe me even if I had told them what he had been doing to me.

The judge's comment, *"But what did he do to you?"* resonated over and over in my head like a scratched record. It was paralyzing to the point that I had sharp chest pains. As the months passed, his covert behaviors escalated. In fact, *"what didn't he do?"* He began sending certified letters to my business address. I never opened them, my friend would read them and only tell me if there was something, I needed to do to protect myself. I was not going to let his nasty degrading comments get into my head and negatively impact my health. Finally, my friends convinced me to hire an attorney. A $10,000.00 retainer was worked out in installments. Using my mortgage money, since my home was in foreclosure, this was the gamble I was willing to take, *all or nothing.* Amid this, I learned Palter had my homeowner's insurance canceled. While trying to get it reinstated, I learned he had me removed from my homeowner's insurance policy, and had me listed as a *"Resident relative."* Huh, why? This becomes relevant and clear later. Finally, a new policy was issued in my name only.

Two weeks later, while at my daughter's house, my car didn't start, I called for a tow, I was shocked to see Plater's name on the receipt. I immediately called Farmers Insurance to discover Palter convinced the agent to put his name back on my homeowner's policy because he wanted a multiple policy discount. Initially, they refused to provide me with the proof of how this took place. After making Farmer's aware that my family would hold them responsible should anything happen to me because he would now be able to falsely gain access to my home, they gave me all of the documents I needed to give my attorney.

My advice, listen to your intuition and instincts, I did, I'm glad I did. Two weeks later Palter and two police officers showed up at my home demanding I let him and the officers in. Remember, that policy, he had his name put back on? Well, he had it in hand. Checkmate, it's no good. I informed the officers this is a civil case not domestic, "You have no jurisdiction" and handed them my cell phone with my attorney on the other end of the line. My attorney told them they needed to leave.

The following weekend my daughters discovered a hidden file cabinet Palter had left behind which contained undeniable proof he had used me the entire eighteen years we were together. There were letters to investors where he acted like my company was his. He used my home as secured collateral for various deals he had made. There were even e-mail printouts of romantic conversations, meetings he had had with numerous women on e-Harmony, reports on their net worth along with their business cards.

Now, more than ever I realized how dangerous and deep his deception was. I made the decision I would continue to fight in the courts in a way he would not expect. Not knowing if I would win or lose, I would admit into evidence as many of these documents that I could. I knew once admitted, they became public record, I would be able to tell my story pulling from public records. I would be able to be believed. Now, he is about to see how a "Naïve" Ivy leaguer operates when pushed.

Every point my attorney needed to make, there was a supporting document in Palter's personal handwriting, signature and/or e-mails. The attorneys had us go to mediation in Santa Monica. Palter refused to negotiate with the judge. However, his attorney approached my attorney in the parking lot and said,…"My client has an offer for your client. He will sign over the house to your client if she signs over the Mama Vega Salsa company to him." I will let you figure out what my attorney said on your own. In legal terms, this is an *illusory* offer. It's an illusion as they are both mine. Next step, back to court.

The hearings lasted three days. In the end, my business remained mine (although I no longer have products in the 100+stores) and the judge granted a Quiet Title (MC024324, 2015), awarding me my home back. I had already negotiated with Wells Fargo for a loan modification (0132103771) without his signature. It took me a year to get the Quiet Title recorded, the county recorder did not "like" how the order was written. What?!? I finally drove to Downey and had it reviewed by a supervisor and recorded (2017).

Within days of the recording, my attorney said he needed copies of my 2015 case and supporting documents because Palter was suing him and me for conspiring against him. I spent my entire Mother's Day weekend scanning two file cabinet drawers. Palter even had someone remove documents from the court files, but he did not count on court transcripts. My attorney won, proved Palter lied. After my attorney finished the fight for his career and livelihood, he informed me that had he lost, both he and I would have gone to jail for seven years for conspiracy. Another *defining moment!*

During this same time, I was trying to refinance my home to make the repairs that were supposed to have been done with the original (2003) refinancing Palter coaxed me to do with him as a cosigner. Without giving you the blow for blow daily battles with potential lenders, roofing companies and more, I uncovered liens against my home initiated by Palter. Another *defining moment!* One lien, not including his personal credit cards originally began as $150,000.00 increased to $256,000.00. *In January 2019, it was* picked up by investors, Park Tree Investments. They refused to negotiate or accept the Quiet Title Judgment or go after Palter for the money. Had I not refinanced with Palter as a cosigner where he made himself a co-owner, my home (4 bd, 4 baths 6 car garage on 1.25 acres) would have been paid off with only taxes each year.

What do you think I did? I'll tell you. I changed my mindset and *decided* to "Let the house go." I did not lose my home, I, chose to "Let a house go". There is a different energy when you *decide* to let something go, verses, feeling you lost something. When there is no feeling of loss, you can move forward with greater ease. Moving on does not mean you forget, what it does mean is, is that you remember the lessons learned, and pass them on so others can have the opportunity to benefit from your knowledge should they choose to listen.

In retrospect, these life situations taught me how to navigate the legal system. It showed me how to set my emotions aside and analyze the facts. I learned how to look and listen to *not what is said,* but *what's not said.* It also taught me how to have a deeper understanding and compassion for women who have gone through these types of situations and encourage women to speak out and *tell the neighbors,* there is no shame. My desire to be an inspiration for other women especially my daughters and granddaughter overshadowed any fear. This allowed me to tap into my other skills; nutrition, culinary, and my natural teaching abilities. My knowledge of nutrition nourished my system giving me the strength and stamina to stay focused. While my culinary skills provided me the additional income to continue the legal fight. In the end, What *He Did ~~To~~ For me* is now helping others. Finally, my friends thought I was joking when I told them God has a sense of Humor, God relocated me to my beautiful home on Cinderella Ave.

About Charmène Vega

Charmène Vega teaches nutrition and cooking classes, born and raised in New York, Vega now lives in California, where she consults for nonprofit and private health organizations. Despite her training as a special education teacher, Vega found she preferred mentoring and teaching abused women and children with disabilities; re-empowering them through nutrition for better health.

Vega has worked with abuse prevention organizations; The Love is Foundation, Healthy Start Program and WIC to name a few. Vega is a member of the American Association of University Women and a Lead Presenter for Ending the Silence – NAMI (National Alliance on Mental Illness). She was nominated for the Athena Award, and was conferred upon an Honorary Doctorate of Humanities for her community works. Vega's mother describes her as one who has always looked to help others; *"while merely a freshman in college, she would drive around with extra food in her car to give to anyone she saw in need."*

Charmène Vega is personally aware, of the scars left by mental, psychological, and emotional abuse which generally leads to some form of physical health concerns. She desires to bring more awareness to these forms of abuse that has often been neglected and ignored by the legal system which focuses solely on sexual abuse. In her case

(MQ009463), she did not have any visible scars, when she went before the judge, the judge asked, "But, what did he do to you?"

To learn more about Vega go to

https://nowchewonthis.blog/upcycledwomen/

and https://mamavega.com

CHAPTER 12

7 Keys to Finally Have a Godly Man

By: Melia Diana

Every failed and broken relationship came to one defiant moment in my life. A point where I surrendered control, allowing Jesus to be my pilot, and me His co-pilot. A point where I allowed Jesus to be my best friend while He brought me my husband. A moment I was determined to be a new woman revitalized in Christ.

I was eliminating the nonsense of narcissism, mediocracy, betrayal, and pompous flattery from boys with peter pan syndrome. I was determined to extinguish unjust treatment after giving my heart and soul away easily, only to leave myself sulking and sobbing in more misery. Boy, I was worn out! (Can I get an AMEN ladies)? Sounds liberating but I'm not going to lie- it was a pruning process.

I had to allow God to step in and fight my battles. He saved me from sins I thought were appropriate. He saved me from a warped image of myself.

As for some of you reading this, I'm sure flashbacks came flooding back into your memory. I'm sure you comprehend the concept of painful breakups. Perhaps, it's hitting a little too close to home for you?

Well, whether it does or not, I was not strong in my faith or walk with Jesus to know any better. I was blinded to the fact the enemy kept me in bondage of sin. I was reliving my past unable to be present in the current. I based all my decisions on fickle feelings and I followed the basic standards and philosophies of an immoral world.

I was always that long-term commitment girl. I invested years with men without a proposal. This time around, I was stepping away from a seven-year relationship to work on revamping myself. I remember it like it was yesterday. This particular toxic relationship was my deal-breaker, my do-over in life.

Every heartbreak, all my tears came down to this pivotal moment where I was ready to listen to what God had to say. I had enough of trying to do it my way which was getting me, nowhere. This time around I got serious about my walk with Christ.

The beach was my special place for reflection and healing; it gave me a chance to spend time with Jesus. Talk to Him. Cry to Him. Be still with Him. Stepping off the beach from cleansing and soul searching, I happened to see a familiar face from a distance. As I approached this friendly face, *BAM*! Another guy came swooping up beside me. We both conjured to ask the same question-at the same exact time. How does that happen? Was this fate?

This is where it started; this man stepped into my life at a time I was trying to detox. We locked eyes with amazement that two strangers had a similar thought process. He was witty, funny, and charismatic but not my typical type. He was tatted up and a bit more unconventional than my usual liking.

And so it began, but there was something not quite right about him. I couldn't put my finger on it. I think at that point; I just wanted some attention from the opposite sex. But *wait*, wasn't I suppose to be alone to heal?

I invested two years into another relationship that didn't lead to marriage. We shared many memories, intimacy, tears, and laughter. We bonded in a special way, but to a point, it became venomous and unhealthy. The illusion that we thought we couldn't live without each other was clearly displeasing. Every time we had a disagreement, he went running to the bars then come banging on my door for a drunken apology. Or better yet, jump on some dating sites. I accepted this twisted treatment. *Why?* I thought I was in love, but does this sound like love? He had multiple so-called girlfriends, which is detrimental when in a committed relationship. This is a *no-no* in my book.

Key Point #1-Both men and women need safe boundaries from contacts of the same sex, in respect of one another.

A man of integrity will show you loyalty by not making you feel you're in competition with another woman.

I thought this man was holy because we went to church and got baptized together. I was blindsided by the immaturity and vanity he presented, assuming because he was older he would have his life better structured. *Nope!* During our courtship, I quickly learned he was not divorced yet and still perusing me. I should have run for the hills at this point- *Big Red Flag!* But I didn't.

Key Point #2- Never get involved with someone straight out a divorce; we all need time to heal from the anger and resentments of our past.

Without healing from any relationship, we will slander our unresolved emotions on the next person, which is not deserved.

The times I did try to work on our relationship it just backfired. I pleaded and tried to communicate to him about things hurting our relationship, but can a leopard take away its spots? (See Jeremiah 13:23). He manipulated me with smooth talk and presented me with gifts and flowers, trying to confess his love for me. He denied me the respect I deserved from a man. But, *wait*! Wasn't I suppose to walk away by now? Why was I holding on?

I have to chime in here and say I was a baby Christian at this point of my walk with Jesus. I was not strong enough in Christ to comprehend how to look for a Christian man. How was I to seek a godly man if I was not exuberating the characteristics of a godly woman? A man chasing God was an abnormality I was not accustomed to view. I was weak.

Key Point #3- Be strong in your faith

At some point we had our hearts broken, torn out of chest, and hung out to dry, leaving us completely devastated. The deep anguish from betrayal, gossip, adultery, and lies is indeed a difficult emotion to overcome. We like to hold onto our emotions, stuff them inside, and then implode with assumptions and misconceptions. This kind of behavior is foolish in God's eyes. "Fools have no interest in understanding; they only want to air their own opinions" (Proverbs 18:2 NLT). Besides pride and ego, why do we allow our past and feelings to dictate decisions for us?

We allow our emotions and affections to rule us and to make resolutions that cloud judgement and overtake us, which is always counterproductive. It's dangerous to live off of our feelings. Since they are constantly changing, why would we base short and long term decisions on them? Think about it...we base our relationships, careers, and our love life from a feeling and then wonder why it collapses if it doesn't work out.

Key Point #4- Don't allow feelings to make decisions for you. As if that's not bad enough, I then ran to friends, family, and psychics for help or advice when it didn't work out the way I wanted it too. *Look,* everyone has a story. Everyone has their own opinion, but their situation is specifically designed for them- NOT you. Seeking feedback from others sources never helps. Why are we not seeking wise council from the creator of the heaven and earth? "If you need wisdom, ask our generous God, and He will give it to you." (James 1:5 NLT).

Key Point #5- Come to God with questions and answers only He can provide.

I can tell you I was ignorant and immature before I came to know Jesus as my personal Savior. Lost and insecure, I ran to everyone for answers instead of God. I craved and idolized the worldly things.

I lived off passion and lust, thinking these fleshy desires were strong enough to carry my romantic relationships to marriage.

Let's be real for a moment. Who doesn't want to be loved and have it reciprocated? That's a given. It's a fabulous feeling, but love is more than an emotion. A lifelong journey take more than gushy butterfly moments. It takes strenuous work. Flaws will prevail, quarrels and disappointments will happen. Growth opportunities will arise, but it's how we respond and our willingness to surrender to Him. Concede to your thinking and look towards God's Word for feedback. Let Him refine you.

We share intimacy and give our hearts away with every potential lover, leaving us frustrated with the embodiment of emotional and psychological damage never sustaining anything fruitful. We jump from relationship to relationship with no real effort to work on changing ourselves. *Yet*, we are told to guard our hearts, not just give them away. "Guard your heart above all else. For it determines the course of your life" (Proverbs 4:23 NLT).

We wonder why nobody makes us happy. If we are honest with ourselves, we should know that it's not someone else's job to make us happy- it is ONLY yours! We must take a look inside ourselves for modifications. Why do we insist on running around in a state of frenzy? Or blame God? "People ruin their lives by their own foolishness and then get angry at the Lord" (Proverbs 19:3).

It's easy to pack up a suitcase, carry our baggage away, and drop our luggage on the next innocent victim. We repeatedly vomit our pain, hurts, and resentments on each other. What good does that do? We carry on like helpless children without any ramifications for some real transformation. We play the victim role, blame, and point fingers avoiding ownership that perhaps something within ourselves is not as healthy as we think. *Look*, we are all hurting, but when will we submit that we played a role in failed courtships? How will we find a partner behaving like that?

Perhaps if we look at the root of our own bitterness, we may indeed find something. *Yikes!* Well, nobody likes to take the sting or pungency of ill-mannerism and vinegariness. If we can ask Jesus to bring our weaknesses in the light with His guidance, He can change these destructive patterns. "Search me, O God, and know my heart; test me and know my anxious thoughts. Point out anything in me that offends you, and lead me along the path of everlasting life" (Psalm 139:23-24 NLT). We cannot do this in our own strength. We all need God to carry us through trials and tribulations. So many times I tried doing things on my own, and time and time again, it blew up in my face.

Key Point #6 Allow God to work on weaknesses hindering your walk.

What if I told you there was a different way to find your man? It is not an earthly way. I'm talking about a spiritual way, stemmed from godly wisdom. The world sure is revolving. The way we look for a man has really lost its charm. Courtship has been exchanged with online dating and text messages. More wallflowers than social butterflies, we hardly speak to each other because our phones have our complete attention. We click on profiles only by a physical attraction. I was guilty of this but I know now that looks alone will not sustain a relationship. We base our ideas of finding a partner by passing judgement, criticizing, and looking for the financial status. *Now*, is this really the way God intended us to find our man?

Living in a fallen world, this makes it more difficult to be a Proverbs 31 Woman. We are told to act, dress, and live up to a standard that society calls normal. A P31W is a woman of integrity. She is a helper for her husband. She is honest, loyal, and compassionate. She has acknowledgment of dying to herself, which is putting others ahead of her. She embodies strength, courage, and tenacity. "She is clothed with strength and dignity, and she laughs without fear of the future" (Proverbs 31:25 NLT). She loves her Abba Father and follows His commandments. She rebukes the enemy in Jesus' name, not allowing Satan to feed her twisting lies and manipulating thoughts.

Does it take time to be like this? *Yes*! Quite frankly, this is a never-ending process. It takes time, persistence, and patience to allow the extension of God's branches to grow. *No*, we won't always get it right. Perfectionism is not required; and we will fall short- that's okay. Get back up and try again; this is what a warrior in Christ does. God gives us grace while your determination won't let setbacks overthrow you.

Ladies, I had to take ownership for my weaknesses. I was blind and insecure. I had no clue what a godly man looked like because I was not a P31W. *Shoot*, I was immature before I came to know the Lord as my personal Savior. My justification for selfishness was to embellish self in everything.

I got serious about finding my husband- a man who is equally yoked. I was on a mission and dead set on cutting out mindless and childish games. This time around, I knew what I was looking for (that pivotal moment I spoke about earlier). I was not going to settle for anything less than the man God intended me to have. I would wait. I was content while Christ opened my eyes. This time I was different. As my relationship grew with Him, He made me strong and courageous. You can have this too!

Key Point #7- Ask God to send your husband.

We all have been though our ups and downs- it's called life. There is usually a hidden lesson is our trials. The bitterness that embodies our soul stems from the damage of sin and toxicity of unresolved feelings. I learned from all my disappointments. Although my ex-boyfriend caused me great grief, I thank him for contributing to my growth and character. I have learned to thank and forgive all my ex boyfriends who hurt me. Without this finale disillusioned link of love, I would have never taken that wholehearted step to the altar.

I struggled with God for years. He had to break me to build me back up. I had to hit rock bottom to pursue Him. Pain is our biggest motivator. It's in our deepest despair, bringing us to our knees when we realize we need to change- to do something different and stop playing the victim role and embrace God's guidance and wisdom.

God can turn our mess into a message. I'm here to tell you that your brokenness can be used and turned into a beautiful blessing for someone else. Let's woman up! Be the P31W God intended you to be. Transformation begins with God but starts with your willingness to surrender. The question is- how bad do you want it?

About Melia Diana

Melia is a wife, mother, writer, and devout Christian woman who loves the Lord. She is indefinitely serious about her faith and walk with Jesus but don't let that intimidate you! She is a well –rounded, robust women exuberating a quirky personality with a twist of funny and compassion.

Melia's entire career has been solely devoted to serve and help others prosper. She has spent over 13 years in the medical & fitness field, and is a faith based Certified Christian Counselor. Melia's unique methodology allows her to utilize her knowledge, experience, faith, and personal development to brand her own business model to detoxify hurting souls. She brings forth what God equipped her and called her to do- to help women spiritually and physically, discover who they are in Christ. Her empathetic approach encourages others for growth and wisdom for a stronger mindset.

In her spare time, Melia enjoys the beach, reading, and spending time with her family. Her heart is focused on the genre of nonfiction Christian writing- with the emphasis on godly relationships and helping women become a Proverbs 31 Woman, which God intended. Melia has published articles with the Good News Newspaper and is actively in pursuit of publishing her new, uplifting, and heartfelt nonfiction Christian book.

For more information, go to her website **meliadiana.com**. You can also find Melia on other social media platforms such as LinkedIn, Pinterest, and Facebook- she welcomes new friends and embraces how God can use her as an extension for His Kingdom.

Blessings xo.

CHAPTER 13

How to Overcome the Modern World by Idolizing an Ancient World Sacrifice

By Maryse Cassamajor

Hello, I am Maryse. If I were in a typical recovery group, I would use word(s) to describe my shortcoming, flaw, or defect. So here it goes -- I am a college-educated, single mother who is homeless.

Traditional recovery groups have helped many people for decades, but I did not find them effective. Before my crisis of faith, I lived life as an idealistic young lady with dreams of changing the world. My college years and adult life significantly impacted my thoughts and choices, which resulted in a major paradigm shift. Today, I write this as a woman of faith - a passionate Christ follower - experiencing single motherhood and homelessness. Do you see the difference? If not, this chapter may help.

Whether you care to admit it, we are created in God's image (Genesis 1:26-27).

With our thoughts, we create our world within and around us. Imagine an 8-ounce glass with 4 ounces of water. Is the glass half-full or half-empty? If the water is being poured into the glass, it is half-full; poured out, half-empty.

I see myself from a position of strength -- I am who God says I am. In contrast, this world, wants to limit me and my potential by reminding me of and seeing me from my worst mistakes. But I think anyone surveying the population would be hard-pressed to find anyone who placed homelessness on their YOLO (You Only Live Once) bucket list, much less, homeless and single motherhood.

My personal situation is complicated, and the solution is complex, but the battle is over. I am just waiting for my outer world to reflect the victory in my inner mind. Jesus redeemed your and my worst mistakes and will transform them into a story to encourage others. Kindly allow me to show you how...

CAUTION TO THOSE LOOKING FOR AN EASY ANSWER

First, spoiler alert... I will not be outlining a quick program or a linear approach to overcome your struggles because my victory didn't take 30 days or a linear path. The life that overcomes challenges and trials -- the life I live - was not and isn't an easy one.

A NOT SO HUMBLE BEGINNING

I am a first-generation Haitian American born in Cambria Heights, Queens, NY. A "first-generation" child is automatically different from the start. My family legally immigrated to the United States and as a first-generation born U.S. citizen, it posed some unique challenges at home and school.

OVERCOMER

Challenges included following the traditional cultural norms of my ethnicity and trying to assimilate into the American culture. Living in Queens made it easier because of the neighborhood enclaves at the time. I think New York is the largest "melting pot" and it is quite evident during the commuting hours. A representative of every socio-economic class and ethnic group gathers in streets, on buses, trains, and subways, to make their way through the urban jungle. It was no different for me growing up.

FIRST LESSONS

I was raised with middle-class values built on a strong foundation of knowing my role within my Haitian household. Since I did not grow up with other Haitian kids, I do not know if my experience is common or atypical. I was seen and not heard until addressed. I learned early on that a grown-up gave you your voice.

This pattern was reinforced further in school through games like telephone and waiting for the teacher to call on you, after raising your hand. In kindergarten, I earned the reputation for being a perfectionist. How, I got really upset when I colored outside the lines. Neither my teacher nor my family tried to remove that trait. I think school reinforces perfectionism for some kids.

Think about it: When do you get a gold star?

What does an "A" grade symbolize?

You get both by being excellent.

As a child, I learned in order to be considered good, you had to be twice as good as the other kids. Getting A's got me praise from my teachers, acknowledgment from most students, and money from my family. Yup, you got paid when you brought home the A's!

STICKS AND STONES...

Being an excellent student made me a recipient for praise, but also of teasing and name-calling. Names like "teacher's pet", "four eyes", and "know-it-all" flew towards me. The word "nerd" had not entered the vernacular, but it would have accurately described me and my fellow classmates.

However, being called "four eyes" did not bother me, initially. Everyone in my family wore glasses. My aunt even worked for an optometrist and eyewear retail store. It was not until a few of my classmates attached a negative connotation to my condition, one that I had no control over changing, that I started feeling bad about wearing glasses.

AN IMPORTANT LESSON LEARNED

Do you know the expression, *"Sticks and stones may break my bones, but words can never hurt me."* Well, for me, it's a lie. Words hurt and being mocked for being different hurts. Being different makes you stand out and, when you stand out, you can be picked on AND applauded. So, I had to learn to accept being picked on and I had to overcome the hurt in order to remain excellent. I wanted, maybe even needed, to be applauded for a job well done.

OVERCOMER

What do you do if the applause does not follow a really good job?

Do you stop pursuing excellence or do you ignore the absence of applause?

A TALE OF TWO STATES

Please, do not get me wrong. School was a positive experience. We treated each other with respect, and we learned the life lessons to toughen up. My best friends were three White boys and when I got bullied, they or other boys would come to my aid to end or report the behavior. Looking back, I had real-life experiences with knights in shining armor.

In addition to social lessons, the New York education system required every child to take Choir, Art, and Physical Education. It makes me sad that these classes are offered as electives today, if at all, but I digress. For me, these classes provided a creative outlet and broadened my education to appreciate the Fine Arts. I learned that I liked being in front of people, whether it was vocal concerts, playing violin in orchestra, marching in the Memorial Day Parade for our community, or providing tips for Junior High success as a graduation keynote speaker.

Unfortunately, these elementary school experiences are sharply contrasted with my middle school experience when we moved to South Florida. First, my math scores placed me higher than the highest-level math class. Second, the "smart kids" were all grouped together, taking the same classes together. While I enjoyed the intellectually stimulating environment, I did not have much interaction with the students I would later call the "resilient" ones.

The resilient ones have to study hard for their grades in school. The resilient ones confront hardships I did not have to face until later on in life. They knew there was more to life than getting straight A's.

In middle school, I encountered racism for the first time when a White boy called me a racially derogatory term for having extra melanin in my skin. It was quite shocking to hear that term from a 12- to 14-year old boy. The boy was not in any of my classes and, apparently, he was angry about where I was sitting in the cafeteria.

However, I was still engaged in an intellectual and competitive environment, both in and out of the classroom, with physical education and music activities for variety. My high school years were more of the same, with the additional pressure to outperform for class rankings, scholarship opportunities, and the bragging rights for highest PSAT, SAT and ACT scores.

AM I "RESILIENT"?

I took the PSAT and learned that my scores did not qualify for the Florida Undergraduate Scholarship. So, my response? I bought preparatory books, gave up my Saturday mornings to attend an SAT study class and memorized college-level vocabulary words. I had the long-term academic track record to indicate success at college (I was excelling at Honors and AP classes) and a high GPA, but my performance on one test, taken on one day, disqualified me for the scholarship I needed to go to college without creating a financial burden on my single mother.

HARD WORK REWARDED, BUT...

I earned the scholarship to attend the University of Florida. It was so exciting being on campus, meeting new people, being truly independent. I quickly made friends with Jennings Hall residents.

We had wonderful times getting acquainted, bonding through our common experience. There was only one major drawback: I was rejected by the Black students for being "too white." Never hearing such a phrase, I heard utterances like "zebra" and "Oreo." The Black boys did not want to date me, so I stuck close to my circle of friends, who happened to be all White males with my best female friend (also White). We were both so innocent, maybe too innocent...

We branched out from our network, started going to fraternity parties on and off campus, and spent nights dancing at the downtown clubs. We enjoyed our newfound freedom and college boys and locals enjoyed our company. Well, things took a turn when the out-of-town girlfriends saw how close we were to their sweet boyfriends. I did not want to cause any unnecessary rifts, so I withdrew from my original group of wholesome brothers and started spending more time with the "revelers".

One night, off campus, things got out of hand with a guy who was a friend of a friend. I lost my virginity that night, something I thought was my most precious asset. I had been drinking and I was at an unfamiliar boy's apartment, so maybe I should have known better. The boy knew of my status, we were "fooling around" and "making out", and I was unfamiliar with the act, so it was pretty much over before I realized what was happening.

Shakespeare said, "nothing is good or bad, but thinking makes it so." So, in my mind, a sexual assault occurred that night. Despite campus campaigns to prevent such occurrences, you will still hear stories of college-aged girls with similar experiences. All unreported. All deemed acceptable and part of the "college experience." All leaving ripples of trauma and reinforcing concepts that women are sexual objects to be enjoyed, conquered, and discarded when the fun is over.

The sexual assault sent me on a tailspin, but I did not have time to focus on it. I had a GPA to maintain to keep my scholarship. I "compartmentalized" the event as a coping mechanism and it was highly effective. So, I utilized it, whenever necessary, in order to accomplish what I needed to get done.

Also, I adopted my own set of rules for sexual activity. I figured since I no longer was a virgin, and no respectable man would ever want to marry me, I might as well enjoy myself according to my rules. It was my feeble attempt to regain some control and it worked for some time... until it did not.

I woke up one day, feeling just as used as that night, except I had a longer list of partners now. And just like that, my promiscuity ended; my coping mechanism failed, and it was time to adopt a new coping mechanism. This "bad girl" had gone good.

OVERCOMER

I had put my past behind me. At least so I thought.

If I allow it, the modern world would have me shrink, even disappear, from the shame of my greatest mistakes. This world wants me grateful for the opportunity to earn back its approval. But I learned a long time ago that I will not be a slave for approval. When you live for man's (or woman's) approval, you subject yourself to the whims of a fickle world that may never ultimately accept you

So, how did I do it?

THE WAY IS PREPARED

I started listening to Christian Contemporary Music (CCM) on my car's radio and cell phone. The stations introduced me to a good mix of classic, popular and breakthrough CCM artists. A Baptist Church gifted me a Daily Walk Study Bible. An Evangelical Church introduced me to the Proverbs 31 First 5 app. I made the commitment to devote several hours each day to seek God.

BEFORE YOU GO FORTH AND MAKE DISCIPLES...

Pastor Michael Patz, Greenhouse Church, says that in order to make disciples, you have to be a disciple first and you do that by seeking God. One can seek God through a variety of ways, but I chose to seek Him by working a home bible study plan, attending formal bible study groups, and devoting my time to worship and prayer.

FINDING MY IDENTITY

I found my identity in "relationship to Jesus," primarily through worship. In worship, I found a love like no other love. I found acceptance for my mistakes and shortcomings. I found that, as God's creation, He saw every day of my life -- the days I got it right AND the days I got it all wrong. And He gave His Son to die on the cross, over 2000 years ago, for my sins so I could be reconciled to Him.

I did not have to do anything to earn it. It was there for me from the time of the earth's formation. All I had to do was accept the salvation as a gift of grace, through faith in Christ alone.

After embracing that love, how could anyone ever go back to the world's fickle nature?

I recall the very moment I encountered Jesus and it was -- you guessed it -- during worship. I was singing Hillsong Worship's, "Christ is Enough." The lyrics started stirring up a commitment to go "all in" with Jesus. I still get stirred up when I reflect on the lyrics:

"Christ is my reward

And all of my devotion

Now there's nothing in this world

That could ever satisfy

Through every trial

My soul will sing

No turning back

OVERCOMER

I've been set free

Christ is enough for me

Christ is enough for me

Everything I need is in You

Everything I need...

The cross before me

The world behind me

No turning back

No turning back

Christ is enough for me

Christ is enough for me

Everything I need is in You

Everything I need (Christ is enough)"

RECOVERY IS POSSIBLE WITH CHRIST

We are all in recovery. NO ONE survives this life unscarred and untouched by the modern world and its snares. The question is whether you are going to base your recovery on a solid foundation of victory or on shaky ground that will inevitably lead to defeat, destruction, and death. My victory is based upon what Jesus did for me on the cross. Today, He continues to care for me, love me, lead me, and remind me continually that I am not alone in trial and victory. He will do the same for you.

About Maryse Cassamajor

Maryse Cassamajor is committed to helping people become passionate followers of Christ. First and foremost, as a mother, she strives to exemplify and impart Christian virtues in her teenage daughter's life. Furthermore, she believes her story will help encourage and inspire others toward a transformational relationship with Christ, where a turning away from destructive and toxic habits gives evidence of the restorative love of God.

Maryse's career in service includes positions in the retail, city and county government, and healthcare industries. Currently, she has plans on becoming a Certified Health and Life Coach. For her, this is a new step of faith. She earnestly desires to serve her community in fresh and innovative ways through this unique opportunity.

After working with chiropractors, Maryse was set on a new path of compassion once she realized that treating patients' illnesses, as she originally intended in her pursuit of a nursing career, was insufficient. She believes that facilitating prevention of illness through community education, services and health industry partnerships is key to improving health conditions in underserved populations. In addition to helping others make healthy lifestyle choices, Maryse aspires to alleviate poverty in her community. She is resolute that when communities invest in themselves, rally together for a common cause, and champion policies and practices that address social inequities, sweeping social transformation can happen in the hearts and minds of its citizens.

Maryse's engaging, yet mildly introverted personality makes listening to others, sharing her insights, and discussing a wide range of topics a mutually enjoyable opportunity to connect.

Let's connect via email at mgcassamajor@gmail.com or linkedin.com/in/maryse-cassamajor .

CHAPTER 14

Trust Your Magic

By: Ana Cristina de Sá

Driving around Miami. How did I get here? How life brought me to this moment? Without knowing I was about to meet two women that were going to be the catalyst to crack me open to reclaim my power and own who I have become. They proved to me that every time I didn't trust my magic, I would suffer the consequences.

Love for the Elements

Born in the vibrant suburb of Rio de Janeiro growing up surrounded by the biological abundance of nature. As a child, I was strong willed, bold, and audacious. Spent most of my time immersed in greenery, climbing trees and being at one with nature.

Happiness was to watch the ants work in unison, the hummingbirds kissing the flowers, the orchard blossoming with tropical fruits. Wearing shoes was irrelevant and combing my hair overrated; some bruises on my legs and arms from falls were worn like battle trophies. In every breath I was whole, I was one and all. It never bothered me that I heard voices, saw energies that others didn't and had premonitions. Didn't seem strange; to me was natural. It was my magic nation - Divine in its most refined expression.

OVERCOMER

<u>Taste of the Urban life</u>

At ten, things changed drastically. Before I could fully comprehend what was going on, we packed and moved to an apartment. Leaving the hanging gardens - ripped away from my oasis. My dog and best friend Susie were given away, my trees, birds, ants, nature were all left behind with a piece of me.

Moved to a world I didn't recognize, surrounded by concrete. Not knowing what to do I would escape to go looking for a park or something that could make me feel at home again. Getting grounded was a daily routine. "You have to play with the other girls." I was told - me "Not the dolls "pretending" games?" Children pretending, adults pretending. All keeping up with appearances. I often thought - "Who are these people?!" Would hear "who do you think you are?" "you are too much of an enthusiast for life that's not good" "life is dangerous, play it safe" "do like everybody else" ... "I must cut your wings"! Those phrases haunted me for years. The echo kept playing over and over in my head. At times and circumstances when I needed the most courage, they paralyzed me.

I started living parallel lives, crossing dimensions all the time. On the surface, attending to urban life, social events, combing my hair, and dressing up fashionably, always feeling like an imposter playing a role that hopefully someday would resume. Unaware I was compromising. For acceptance, I stifled and limited myself. Was projecting a veil that was pleasurable to others but false to myself.

Walking away from my authentic self, my memories of oneness with life were fading. Behind the veil, I cried.

Out of fear I kept trying to stay in the box assigned to me living with a longing for authenticity, and a desire to break free. "This world is no place for an enthusiastic free spirit" I was told. Against my inner nature, I continued to conform with the status quo, that would make "society" happy, I thought. Would I be happy? For a while it worked and I became quite good at the game of fitting in.

Now living in a beautiful house, I got my first car, my own room and we had more maids. Got into college and on my way to becoming a perfect trophy wife. Life was easy and convenient. I had gotten comfortable pretending, even though I would go in and come out of depression silently. Arguing with myself that there was no reason to be depressed that giving up on our essence was "normal" it was part of growing up, everybody was doing it. Why would I be different? Why would I want to be unique?

Life Surge

As a young adult, life caught up with me and my world would never be the same. My emotional, sentimental and financial worlds collapsed overnight. No north star, no point of reference, no disclosure, just everything around us crumbling. Many things were hidden and or unsaid came to life. Found out my "hero" father had another family for years and had lost everything leaving us broken in ways I wouldn't even be able to express. In the cascading anger, blame and chaos that followed, it was like an avalanche that swallowed us. I didn't know which way was up, which way was down. Our lives changed so dramatically, hit so hard, so cold, and so abruptly, that I could barely breathe.

1997 the USA. After years of a "perfect life", unspoken and unnoticed depression my world had crushed on me. I had gone from a wild free child that believed combing her hair was overrated and wearing shoes irrelevant to a spoiled and conformist lost young woman. With the distractions and promises from society I no longer stood up for my freedom or uniqueness. If everything was fine before, you may ask: Why the depression? Compromising and betraying my essence was the monster in my closet.

Now what? I didn't know how or who to be without the lifestyle it was created for me. Beautiful clothes, cars, big house, neighbors that just looked like us. Who are the Joneses? Were we the Joneses? Felt like a movie, a bad one. I was living someone else's life instead of becoming the woman I should be.

Destiny called, in the middle of all this chaos a friend invited me to move to Boston with her. I took my chance. Sold my bedroom furniture and moved with enough money to last me probably a month. Arriving in Boston was refreshing; so many new things, the first time I was on my own. Working as a waitress and going to school I enjoyed meeting new people that were completely different from me. Enrolling myself in one of the most prestigious schools in the world to expand my horizons. I hung out with brilliant eager young minds from many parts of the world, tasted all kinds of international cuisine, heard music played by legends at Berklee, discussed science and religion with MIT and Harvard professors. Freedom and expansion were knocking on my door.

Then from nowhere I started shrinking into the old belief system that I must play safe and conform. My thoughts went to "If I worked hard enough, then the family will re-integrate." "If I stop questioning life, behave properly, complied with what was expected of me, the situation at home would improve, and everything would be back to normal." "If I stay with the programing everything is going to be okay again." My inner child was full of guilt and shame for being out playing while the rest of the family was still picking up its pieces.

I wanted badly to be the savior of the family. Kept myself busy entertaining opportunities that were never aligned with who I was nor my talents. Again, I was afraid to be myself. In the meantime, my psychic powers and extraordinary experiences would manifest in daily visions, flashes of insight, and nightly dreams, I was embarrassed to admit them. I suppressed the Sacred within me in favor of a superficial pleasant-looking exterior. Kept my prophetic insights to myself for fear of being labeled as "crazy".

I was in a hurry, going nowhere. My activities were done halfheartedly, born from a place of "monkey mind" chatter. I'd start one project, only to veer off halfway, undone, into another project. I knew I needed to redirect but didn't. Still compromising, trying to "fit in" - trying to create this perfect persona envisioned by my family. Living out of alignment had begun to catch up with me psychosomatically. I needed to take care of myself. I was either super happy or depressed experiencing strong pains in my body and developed a fibroid in my uterus that almost took my life.

The return to myself

Rushed to the hospital and waking up from an emergency surgery, I was put on home rest for two long months. In this time of reflection - the break I needed - the universe conspired to *finally* have me slow down, tune in, and listen to my heart's desires.

Only at death's door did I begin to appreciate the impermanence of life. In the process of almost losing it, I realized that I had to dance to the beat of my own drums. I dove back into spirituality- with two feet this time! - and began to find my center. Starting my way back to my essence. Changing course re-learning what I was communing with as a teenager. Embracing what I went through, I found the compassion to forgive myself for leaving my essence behind.

Through meditation and studying I began hearing pearls of wisdom, allowing it to take root in my heart. They say "When the student is ready the teacher will come." A-ha moment realizing "I cannot wait for someone else to turn my light on, I must be the one turning the switch." During this time, I began receiving high-frequency thoughts. These would manifest as feelings of knowing and premonition. For the longest time I was disconnected with that part of me. The part I believed was weird and needed to be repressed... No, not anymore!

My viewpoint on my abilities were transmuting. Evolving the self is an act of compassion and love. I had a gift. Like rays of divine sunlight breaking through dark clouds, I came to appreciate the miracle of life that was manifesting all around me. When I turned that switch on, I allowed myself to *be the light* - I could breathe again.

Desiring a deeper level of change, it was time to honor my feminine energy. Having been operating from a survival mode, for years I cultivated the masculine energy and was hard on myself. It was now the moment to connect with mother's earth love that served as a feminine grounding point to integrate my energies becoming **BioSacred**.

"An apple tree knows it's an apple tree. The tree is not confused." I needed to find where my seed originated from. I needed to become like the apple tree. I needed to find my family of light. Time was due for me to get in touch with my 'I' self. There I went into the unknown once more. Miami, a city between the North and South Americas with open arms, music and beaches to receive me.

Once in Miami, my psychic abilities and sensitivity got stronger. My intuition reached new heights. Not knowing how to live this new reality, feeling alone and disconnected, I prayed, I chanted, I studied, I meditated. Trips to the mountains, the deserts, fasting, shamanic ceremonies etc. My goal was to fully commit and connect with my essence. So I did, it was a long way since the first stage of my awakening. It was the beginning of a new era, the "Super Spiritual Me"!

OVERCOMER

I was so "spiritual" that I reached a patamar where I was creating the belief that 'whoever wasn't working on their spiritual life wasn't expanding their consciousness.' I was judging. By judging others, I was still judging myself. Red flag- Right there was a warning sign that I was still unbalanced. Who was I to decide or to assume how one's consciousness is? With that realization I dropped my judgments of myself and others and continued my life's quest.

With love and wisdom, I embraced my ego and my shadows as much as my light. I held my inner child with the deepest respect and appreciation. Showering her with bliss, forgiveness, acceptance expressing with my heart, soul and whole body how much I missed her. That was my communion of the mind, body and spirit of our **BioSacred** Trinity, the alignment that connects us to the whole.

Miami with its blue sky, white sand beaches encourages me all day, everyday to come out of my comfort zone, to take responsibility for my happiness. Living the paradox of stillness in motion. Staying present in my life while getting out of my own way. Honoring my sacred self and healing at my own pace. **<u>Unapologetic BioSacred</u>**

Taking my power back I embraced my weakness and saw that I could turn it into a strength. I managed to "air bend" the challenges life was throwing at me, and positively make a change for the better. I didn't have to say goodbye to the person I was; I merely needed to have the courage to step into the type of person that I wanted to become now.

A Sacred life isn't a perfect one. A Sacred life is just life lived at its fullest with its ups and downs. Nourishing our mind, body and spirit at each inhale and exhale. Allowing my life to unfold made me ready for what was next: assisting others to reconnect with their **BioSacred** selves. Bringing harmony, life, and love to those I encounter everywhere anywhere. Finding awesomeness through self-awareness. Today I live with that warm memory in my heart, that freedom of beingness, that enriching simplicity found in nature. An apple tree knows that it is an apple tree. The tree is not confused.

Resistance to change is a fear-based reaction to life's expansion. Our lives happen in the connections we experience in our world. The interconnection between ourselves and our environment is our reality. One of the aspects of our spiritual journey is the unlearning of fear and the acceptance of love. The trees lose their leaves every year to get them all back a season later. Life has its flow and knowing how to surf and embrace it makes our time traveling in this realm much more enjoyable and richer. That is faith ... That is alignment with life's intelligence ... That is trusting in the divinity of our lives. That is to be **BioSacred**.

We are always traveling from one breath to another. We don't want to waste our breaths, do we? We wouldn't want to live our lives in a hurry going nowhere, would we? So why do so many of us keep chasing our dreams as if they were carrots in front of us? Let's honor our past, value our present and embrace the unfolding.

OVERCOMER

The one who keeps his integrity and adapts evolves. The one who knows himself is powerful. Be the principal participant in your life, dance with it, be malleable; welcoming changes that are indeed inevitable and necessary. Life is a stream of consciousness traveling through time and space in order to learn from itself, create and expand; we are it. Our soul's journey brings us to the BioSacred Space where life happens and flourishes in the now.

I travel this life's journey consciously allowing events and people to change me. Now I choose how this alchemical process is done by empowering and loving myself; always evolving into a better version of me. That's how I became the woman of my dreams.

With love,

A.C.

Ana Cristina de Sá

Founder & Provocateur of BioSacred

Transpersonal Intuitive Coaching

Brand Energy Consulting

Space Harmonizing

www.biosacred.com

email: me@biosacred.com

Instagram: @biosacred

About Ana Cristina de Sá

Ana Cristina is a speaker, a writer, and lifestyle expert. Originally from Rio de Janeiro, she moved to Boston in 1997 where she worked with ivy league scientists and professors to bridge the gap between eastern spiritual practices, modern science and marketing. After 16 years of freezing winters, she finally decided to return to warmer climates, sunny beaches and her Latin culture in Florida.

Her work in Boston combined with the community that she built in Florida led her to found BioSacred. BioSacred is a transformational transpersonal program dedicated to empowering people to unapologetically live their truth and create vibrant, joyful lives. It combines marketing, science, psychology, and spirituality.

With BioSacred Ana Cristina has integrated her marketing background with her lifetime of experiences, spiritual studies and psychosynthesis coaching methodology (an approach to psychology focused on personal growth— of personality integration and self-actualization with transpersonal development— of inspired creativity, spiritual insight, and unitive states of consciousness). Ana helps her clients to connect with their deepest callings and directions in life by aligning their lives and businesses with their larger vision and equipping them with the tools to bring it to life. Trust your magic is her mantra.

OVERCOMER

When she's not transforming her clients' lives, she is giving extra hugs and kisses to her dog Panda and cat Mimi, or recharging in nature.

Ana Cristina de Sá

email: me@biosacred.com

phone: 305.951.1009

webpage: www.biosacred.com

instagram: @biosacred

facebook: BioSacred

CHAPTER 15

OVERCOME THE PAIN AND ENJOY THE SUCCESS

By Carolina Marin

God's timing is always perfect. There is no better moment to be writing than right in the middle of the crisis we are currently experiencing due to the Covid-19 Outbreak.

How to Overcome this situation?

Let me give you my perspective. It is not right nor wrong. But it is my hope that after you read this chapter you feel inspired to become a better version of yourself and to create better results.

Many of us will *overcome* this transition by adjusting to it and even foreseeing new opportunities for a brighter future. Those will be *'The Victors'* – sounds like ancient Rome.

Others won't choose to look at this situation with that same perspective. This second group will allow themselves to be overwhelmed and will let their scarcity mindset respond negatively to their inevitable reality. This group will become *'The Victims'*.

I will share something with you: How we view things changes things.

Let's just put it this way; there is no coincidence that you are reading this chapter of this book now, dear *Overcomer.* You are reading it because, you too my friend and courageous entrepreneur believe that, you have the ability to BE more, DO more and HAVE more. You belong to the first group. You make things happen!!

I have always believed that to be true in my life: Count me in!

I would always say that statement fearless and enthusiastically, failing at times to be my word. Shortly after affirming it, obstacles and difficulties would get in the way, and I would decide it was 'too much work' or 'too difficult' for me. I was not good enough, intelligent enough or persistent enough…and I would give up halfway into it. That pattern of thinking and behaving would stop me from getting to my reward.

Have you ever felt that too? (Reflect and respond)

_____

_____

_____

_____

_____

_____

This is going to surprise you, but I am no longer where I was then. I *overcame* self-sabotage, a scarcity mindset, and a victim mentality. I was able to de-construct what I knew about myself and the world and became a successful business owner with multiple income streams. How did I go from not believing in myself to conquering my dreams? This is the exciting part…

I am going to take you on a journey of how I re-found my true self. Coming from a background of entitlement, being raised in a family of three with multiple years between us and in a country that reinforced limiting beliefs and complaints as a lifestyle. I was able to get out of the system and *'Voilá'* I succeeded. It was not easy. Not a bit. Indeed, it was painful. Very. Growth is painful. But the reward is immensely gratifying.

I will share with you WHO and WHAT my turning point was to then provide you with a **3 Success Step System** that is very simple to grasp but it took me enormous amount of intentionality to accomplish.

I promise you something. If you follow this system and apply it to your life you will achieve success and a high amount of riches in many areas of your life.

That is right!

Success can be translated into this system when we truly understand that consistency compounds. Please do not make the same mistake I did. I spent years of my life overestimating the power of tomorrow and underestimating the power of today. The first time I heard John Maxwell speak he said these words and they sank in my heart like fire, leaving a mark…*Today Matters* is a great book he wrote that I recommend.

One of the best parts about my journey is being able to share it. if I have the opportunity to inspire and to encourage you to think that you have what it takes to be an *overcomer,* only if you continue to believe in yourself then there is nothing greater. This is my 'Why' to write this chapter.

There is something I consider necessary to overcome any situation in life and be successful: **Rewire Your Mind.**

I came to the world as an unexpected gift. I was always told so. My dad was 40 years old and my mom 36 when they had me. Back in the 80's that was considered 'too late for a baby'. My mom would always say, *"Sweet Carolina, the baby of the house."* At school I felt embarrassed because my classmates would point at my mom and say, "Is that your grandma?." When my older sister would come around I would occasionally lie and say she was my mother…As the baby of the house I enjoyed the many perks that came with it; extra money and gifts from everyone. I did not have to fight for curfew as a teenager as my older sister did…Soon I learnt that, as long as I would get good grades at school and be responsible, I could get away with anything. At that moment it felt great, but as an adult I ended up paying the price for this lack of discipline. I needed to *rewire my mind* and let go of my childish behavior.

Fascinating diversity, vast variety of culture, equally varied food that provide yet another exciting aspect to a greater experience, friendly and warm people willing to make you feel loved and have the best time…that is Spain. It is a wonderful country and I am proud of being born and raised there. We do know how to live life well. One drawback of Spain is the tendency to reinforce limiting beliefs into its citizens that grow feeling entitled to receive help. This fact influenced me and led to the development of a scarcity mindset. Whenever I would see myself thinking big, I would default to the common phrases:

-Who do you think you *are?*

-Money does not grow on *trees.*

-Money is the root of all *evil.*

-Rich people are *corrupt.*

-Get a real *job.*

The country and family where I grew up made me who I was until I faced a turning point.

At the end of my twenties I felt entitled. I was entitled to receive the best treatment wherever I went and whoever I spoke to. I was entitled to be respected, admired and followed. I was used to getting great results because I understood from an early age that the right attitude could make me more effective when dealing with people. However, entitlement and lack of discipline were the culprits of my limits.

One of my first adventures abroad was to enjoy six months in charming and enchanted Prague as an Erasmus student. Erasmus is a scholarship that allows European students to study abroad in other countries of Europe. It was such an amazing and eye-opening experience that transformed my life. It was wild, too. Being born and raised in Madrid I was forced to learn English due to the profession I choose at the time. I decided to become an English teacher and I had to learn the language. I lived in Prague for a semester and the following year I moved to England.

During that time, I started to become aware of certain resistance that was foreign to me…it kind of got in the way…I have heard others say that what you **resist shall persist** so my way to overcome that resistance was to increase my awareness that I was being entitled. I entered a bookstore in beautiful Prague to buy a planner. It was an antique place and it reminded me of a scene of the movie *The Diary of Anne Frank*. 'Good morning' I said. 'I need a planner'. The person behind the register did not understand a word, replied in Czech and turned her back to me. The same incident happened a couple of times; in a restaurant and at another store. I was so frustrated. 'I get that they do not speak English, but how can they be so rude?' I was upset. I understood firsthand *Miguel de Unamuno's* quote: *"Nationalisms are cured by travelling."* Not that I was ever a nationalist, quite the opposite, but the quote made total sense.

My experiences in Prague and England helped me to understand that I was entitled to nothing and that everything required hard work, discipline and my strongest strength: a good attitude. It was not until I came to the US that my life really had a major turning point in terms of learning who I really was.

Despite my upbringing and my belief system I could manage to *Rewire my Mind* for success. And the best of all is that, if I could do it then you can too. You lack no abilities.

I came to Florida to teach Spanish. My biggest motivation was to travel around the vast US, meet new people and be immersed in the culture I learnt from Hollywood movies. God had different plans for me. Little did I know, what I thought was another 'outward' experience turned to be an 'inward' journey to discover myself and my purpose.

I met my #1 mentor and love of my life, to whom I owe much of what I have accomplished so far; my loving and wise husband Roland. When I met him everything about him was so fascinating! Five years later, everything about him still attracts me. He led me to God and has been guiding me in the process of finding my own self and rewiring my mind.

As I increased my awareness through painful growth experiences – that's right, growing is painful. I realized that for a long time I tended to put the blame on others because it is easier than to face my own shortcomings and irresponsible behavior.

Letting go of some patterns of thinking and behavior was necessary since they were keeping me captive to become the person who I needed to be to conquer my dreams. Of course, resistance came knocking on my door.

My biggest challenge is to lead myself. "Why do you look at the speck of sawdust in your brother's eye and pay no attention to the plank in your own eye?" Matthew 7:3. The Bible shares real truths.

OVERCOMER

It does take an incredible amount of intentionality but if you are successful at *rewiring your mind,* nothing will ever stop you.

Now that I have taken you through the importance that it is to know who you really are, your strengths, weaknesses and letting go of what does not serve you to Rewire your Mind, let me introduce you to the **3 Success Step System** that all entrepreneurs should follow to find success:

1. Identify Opportunity

This, my friend is **KEY** to success. All successful people I know have **CREATED OPPORTUNITIES**. As I look back in my life, I could see how I identified and created opportunities to make my wishes happen. Even though I did not grow in a family or a country who would encourage me to think big, this came innately to me. I got my first job when I was 16. I used to work delivering newspapers in my town. It felt good to make money and experience a sense of freedom; I did not have to ask my parents for permission to do or buy things. I was *creating* my own way. I was at high school at the time. I took part in bad habits during the weekend. My friends and I would do 'botellón' which is to drink as much as you can in a park during a couple of hours to then go to clubs. I would also smoke pot. The weekends seemed like double work for me; I would go out and party and the following day study and prepare for the week at high school. As I mentioned early in the book *'Count me in'* was ingrained on me. I even got a certificate at a summer camp that said: *'Carolina, la que se apunta a un bombardeo'* which means "I would sign up for everything!"

I did not want to miss out on the fun, the boys, and the party and the being high. Despite my circle of influence, my responsibilities were not neglected. I was smart enough, thank God to know that I had to go to College and I did! That same behavior continued throughout my Erasmus experience and into the year in England. The responsible Carolina would show up for the exam, for the project and for the next *opportunity* to travel and live abroad. While others were only seeing fun and pleasure, I would do the hard work to follow my dreams. My friend Elvira, who I adore and met in Prague would always tell me *"Carol, how can you go to bed drunk at 5am and go to class at 9am?"* I still remember that 40 min commute from my dorm to Celetna, the square in Prague where my university was…and by then I didn't use to drink coffee, can you imagine that?

What I am conveying through my story is that, opportunity is always there.

All you need is to find it and make it happen!

Be intentional about the people you talk to.

Who can help you get to where you need to go?

And this only works if you are willing to serve others first.

I dislike when people say this about successful people: *"He has always been lucky…"* What? There is no such thing as luck. Those at the top know this very well. **Luck is when preparation finds opportunity**. It means that you have been sowing so many seeds that you can remember. And only then, there will come the abundant harvest.

The problem is that I now live in a culture where instant gratification is an expectation. That is why too many have the faulty belief that just by taking a tiny bit of action they will produce miraculous results. Then come the complaints, 'That did not work for me...'. Let me tell you that you cannot plant a seed and eat the fruit the same day.

This is a good moment to practice this wisdom, Albert Einstein said: 'In the middle of adversity lies opportunity.'

What opportunity is waiting for you in this crisis? (Reflect and respond)

_____

_____

_____

_____

_____

_____

2. Follow your intuition.

Intuition is a faculty of the mind. How often do you use it?

I have been faced with so many decisions to make in my life that have led me to where I am today. I faced opposition when trying to accomplish big things. It was risky to go and study abroad in another country, I did it. It was risky to enter a multilevel marketing company, I did it. Several years ago, I was given the opportunity to join a direct sales company of essential oils, Young Living. What I saw as a great way to rise, my husband saw as a scam and pyramid scheme. I made the decision based upon my intuition and I pursued it. Now I enjoy a life of wellness and a shared vision with a team of wonderful people: we help people to achieve wellness, purpose and abundance. I followed my intuition, what I call **God's whisper**. And I am so happy I did.

Another time I followed my intuition and faced opposition was when I decided to invest in a high price certification to become a coach with the John Maxwell Team. At the time, Roland and I had just moved into our new house and I was working as an elementary teacher. It was risky for me to invest a large amount of money into a certification, but I knew that decision needed to be made. I was hungry for knowledge and resources that would equip me to become a better leader in order to empower others. I followed my intuition, got on a payment plan and did it. Now I am in a position to equip business leaders and entrepreneurs with the necessary leadership skills to create a vision and improve their bottom line. Had I waited on it…it would have never happened.

Even my decision to write the chapter of this book. I followed my gut! One side of me was telling me it is just not the time. Had I not, you would not be learning the system of success!

You too, might probably be wondering whether this is the right time to make that next move. Choices and decisions are one thing that successful people are very good at and here is when you need to follow your gut. When it comes to a bigger purpose, your calling…do not allow opposition or fear stop you. I am a person of faith so I would encourage you to listen to God's whisper and ask Him:

What do you want me to do? (Reflect and respond)

_____

_____

_____

_____

_____

_____

If you acknowledge Him in all the things you do, He shall direct your path.

Excellent ideas or opportunities are not enough. Nothing comes merely by thinking about it. Action needs to be taken. If not, nothing happens!

Where are your results?

Who has your money?

3.   Execute without fear

This is the most important step in the 3 Success Step System! If you want to achieve success you need to act, get things done, follow through on your ideas and plans. This is the difference between those who get to the top and those who don't. Individuals in this last group tend to postpone doing things until it is too late. They spend too much time thinking about whether they should do it or not.

I grew up thinking a great attitude was everything. I was wrong. Yes, attitude is important, but I have to put the work into the dream plan. Something that reveals different personality characteristics and an assessment I've used is the DISC profile. Through it, I learned that I am a high "I" (promoter, influencer). I am able to inspire and motivate others and myself towards action easily. The challenge is that it wears off and I do not like to put the work in that it takes to complete my goals. This is an attitude for failure. ***Success requires great amounts of action.***

I have good news. The more action you take the more confidence and momentum you will build. Apart from more income, inner-security and self-reliance.

It might be scary to take that first step, but you will be happy to know that the way we overcome fear is by taking action. In my entire life, every time that I made up my mind to achieve a goal God has always given me the resources that I needed to make it happen. You will come up with ways to accomplish your goal.

Of course, we need to be aware of the obstacles and difficulties that will get in your way of you accomplishing the goal. Count on them. If you really want to be successful you will become a master at problem solving and will manage to find solutions as these problems arise. Your capacity for resilience will surprise you!

All human beings share certain addictions that will get in the way of your execution. Be aware of them, examples:

-Being right

-Being comfortable

-Looking good in front of others

Every time you set a goal to accomplish, these will show up and the root of them is fear. Fear brings doubt and when we doubt ourselves, we fail. I encourage you today to take massive action despite fear. Failure is necessary for success, so count on it. It will happen. We must learn from failure in order to move forward!

Rewiring your mind and applying the 3 Success Step System into your life will require intention and effort. But I promise you that, like I did, you will be able to think creatively, learn to listen to God's whisper and overcome any fear or circumstance and success will be at your fingertips.

The chapter does not end here. Schedule a Rewire Strategy Consultation today so we can create a plan that propels you to become the person who can create opportunities and make them happen. Take action!

About Carolina Marin

As a Spanish transplant in the United States, Carolina's journey began as an educator in Madrid. After earning her Master's degree and teaching for a solid ten years, her passion evolved into a desire to pivot that skillset to teach entrepreneurs and business leaders growth strategies, leadership skills and effective communication through 1-on-1 coaching, leadership workshops and seminars.

She generously shares her own leadership journey and discoveries with those who hunger for personal growth and business growth. There is nothing more satisfying to Carolina than the opportunity to inspire and encourage others to believe they have been created for greatness; they have what it takes to overcome any obstacle in their path to success.

Carolina is known as a dynamic and energetic Transformational, Leadership Coach and Public Speaker who is able to turn a full room into inspired individuals and challenge their limiting beliefs to paradigm shift their lives and position themselves for success, having won the greater part of the battle occurring in the mind.

In order to reach your full untapped potential as a business or individual, a *"Rewiring"* transformation process must take place in your mind and thinking.

OVERCOMER

As a certified Trainer, Coach and Speaker with the John Maxwell Team, Carolina is qualified to take you or your business to the next level on your own personal *Rewire Journey.*

She has designed a 3 Step Success System that describes how she went from a place of entitlement, scarcity mindset and unfulfillment to becoming a successful business owner with multiple income streams.

"Once you ruthlessly set the intention to create transformation and progress you are already halfway there.

Let me guide you through the rest."

~Carolina

EPILOGUE

By Wendy Elliott

June 2020, would we ever have thought that we would just be getting through one of the most physically and mentally challenging as well as completely confusing times of our lives?

Although history shows that there has been a pandemic almost once every 100 years, this is the first that our generation has seen that has had such an impact on our daily life, our normal ways of doing things, changing our very ability to be free to do as we please. But, as I continue to ponder what is to come now, I also wonder if the old normal is where we want to be nor should be. Nationally, locally, and all over the globe there has been fear, uncertainty about what will happen next, and how to get through all of this and be the country, family, and person that we were before. Although there is darkness still in our world, the good news is that there has also been such an outpouring of Love, of Hope and of Appreciation showing that there is a culture that can be kind and caring.

Websters dictionary describes the word *Overcomer* as, "A person who succeeds in dealing with or gaining control of some problem or difficulty." How apropos is the timing right, as we release the book Overcomer?

There are remnants and signs that we can and will **OVERCOME** this pandemic, as well as its trials and tribulations and be better than ever. Better than we ever thought we could be. We will just have to choose to do so and lean in on HIM to guide us.

As **Elite Foundation's publisher** releases **Overcomer,** the last book in this series of *Inspired Stories of Real People with Unconquerable Will to Thrive and Be Alive,* we cannot be more in line with **Thriving** and having **Unconquerable Will** can we?

There are no coincidences, this planned series based on four significant words, and the dates of their release were predestined. God had designed even these small details long ago and knew exactly how He was guiding us. Each year as Elite Foundation published its titled books, FEARLESS, INVINCIBLE, and UNSTOPPABLE, we saw His presence in the timing, the culture of where we were as a world, and where we were headed. He knew!!

Acts 1:7

He said to them, "It is not for you to know times or epochs which the Father has fixed by His own authority".

Psalm 139:4

Even before there is a word on my tongue, Behold, O Lord, You know it all.

Elite's collaborative book program is key to the Foundation's success, it is not only a medium to obtain funds for freedom, but it has honored us with the privilege of working with amazing individuals whose stories are the secret to their success, as well as for others. Royalties from Elite Foundation publisher allow for the provision of scholarship awards for those survivors that would not be able to tell their stories otherwise.

Elite Foundation Publisher wants to acknowledge and praise all 55 of the amazing stories, and the exceptional writers that shared their stories even though often painful and hard to impart. Elite Authors, you were all inspiring and brave. Your authenticity and vulnerability are only outmatched by your zeal to not only succeed but to fund freedom for survivors who are still in the grips of pain and abuse that need so desperately to hear your message of **HOPE.**

The book **Overcomer** did not only share the author's unique experiences but equally as important they will illuminate Light into the darkness, instill hope to the wavering and offer strategies and solutions to navigate some of life's most difficult occurrences.

Revelation 3:2

He who overcomes, I will grant him to sit down with Me on My throne, as I also overcame and sat down with My Father on His throne.

Wendy L. Elliott MBA/HCM, M.A. CCC-SP

Multiple Best Seller and Publisher

Elite Foundation, Co-Founder/COO

Coach and Advocate

ELITE FOUNDATION. EDUCATE. EMPOWER. EVOLVE.

VISION STATEMENT
A FUTURE FOR EVERY SURVIVOR

EliteFundsFreedom.org   #ItEndsWithUs   #EndHT

NOTE OF APPRECIATION

The saying, "It takes a village" could not be a more accurate description of Elite Foundation's operant philosophy. The Foundation is a 501(c)(3) nonprofit organization that stands in the gap to educate, empower and to help others evolve their full potential to become Warriors for Change. By investing in yourself and in our goods and services, know that you are funding freedom for those who need our help most.

All royalties from our goods and services fund lifesaving services that are part of Elite's *Pathway to Their Freedom.* For more information about our community services please visit www. EliteFundsFreedom.org

The Foundation is able to expand the work that it does with survivors of human exploitation in all its ugly forms and victims of sex trafficking, due to the generosity, integrity and commitment from all our trustees, board members, community partners, donors, volunteers and you, the socially conscious consumer.

Each of our collaborative books in our world class international bestselling series features dozens of writers, who like you had a dream to become an author, and an impactful message to share with the world. We would like to thank each contributing author for their authenticity, transparency and contribution to the literary work in Overcomer. Each author is a **Thriving-Survivor and Warrior for Change**.

Our production services that include indie publishing and content creation are predicated on the belief that your story matters and that storytelling is the **Key to Your Success**. If you have an interest in sharing your story, we are happy to receive a request for consideration by writing to: ElitePublisher@EliteFundsFreedom.org

Subsequent to receipt of your request for a consultation, our dedicated literary staff will contact you, provide a NDA and walk you through the next steps to becoming an author.

We would like to extend a warm Thank You of appreciation to our production team members, who specialize in working with writers, who are at different stages of the writing process.

Whether you are interested in being a contributing author in one of our collaborative world class international bestselling book series, or you have a book idea, or a developed concept, we have the tailored service that will meet your need.

On behalf of Wendy Elliott, the co-founder of Elite Foundation, and myself, Dr. Jessica Vera thank you for purchasing our goods and services. Know that it takes just $4.11 a day, to set a survivor on the **Pathway to Their Freedom.**

Onward and upward Warriors!

#ENDHUMANEXPLOITATION
#ENDHUMANTRAFFICKING #ITENDSWITHUS

Made in the USA
Monee, IL
30 May 2025

18132796R00108